THE *YOU* YOU'VE NEVER MET

COMPANION JOURNAL

This belongs to:

_____

If found, please respect the privacy of its contents
and immediately contact:

_____

CONTENTS

EMSO INVESTIGATIONS:
The *You* You've Never Noticed

EMSO REPAIRS:
The *You* You're Revealing

EMSO MASTER CHARTS

Welcome,

I'm so glad you've found your way to EMSO (Emotional Sobriety) Training and a unique community ready to support you on your journey.

This journal was designed as a companion to both its mother book, "The *You* You've Never Met," and the "EMSO Essentials" intensive or self-led courses. Its purpose is to give you the space and organization that the book alone could not. It contains all of the required "Take Action" exercises in the curriculum, as indicated with a ⓣ, as well as multiple copies of the EMSO Master Chart in the back, noted with Ⓜ.

Please only complete these exercises in the timing and order that is requested of you in the book or course you're taking. Once you complete a Take Action, do not go onto the next unless it's recommended in the curriculum, which contains the required information to assist you in successfully completing each one. Your journey to Emotional Sobriety using the book/course and journal combined will be much more effective if you do so!

EMSO Training specifically requires a fair amount of writing. Why? I believe that when we write, we are teaching ourselves—the different parts of our brain—in a variety of ways that are otherwise unattainable through only reading or speaking. When we write, we are taking literal action for our transformation. We are creating new patterns and building new synapses in our brains. Think of writing as reviewing and recording your past patterns, while inscribing and authoring your new life.

The EMSO Essentials curriculum is the inward journey, and is organized in 3 Parts:

- **FOUNDATIONS**—**awareness** of your Anatomy of Emotional Insobriety and the *you* you've been being.

- **INVESTIGATIONS**—**acknowledgment** of the *you* you've never noticed.

- **REPAIRS**—continued **acknowledgment** of the *you* you're revealing.

The **action** and **application** to put this into practice in your relationships and truly attain Emotional Sobriety, is available as a follow-up curriculum called EMSO Practicum.

Remember, when you hit points of resistance and challenge, recommit to doing this work, remember why you're here, and choose **the next right thing.**

Always here for you,

Dr. Andrea Vitz

LEVELHEADEDDOC.COM

ANATOMY OF EMOTIONAL INSOBRIETY

GRAPHICS

ANATOMY OF EMOTIONAL INSOBRIETY GRAPHICS

Throughout your EMSO Training, you'll use the following series of graphics to help identify various parts of your emotional insobriety. These are all based on the research done in my practice over many years, and represent the most common forms of each aspect of emotional insobriety, including:

- Common Early-Age Traumas
- Common Trauma-Influenced Self-Beliefs
- Common Trauma Filters
- Common PANEs (Predominant Accompanying Negative Emotions)
- Common ETBs (Emotionally-Triggered Behaviors)
- Common Motives

You will refer back to these once you begin the work. For now, skip ahead to the first Take Action on page 16. Each Take Action in the first section (which also appears in the book) will allow you to increase awareness of the *you* you've been being.

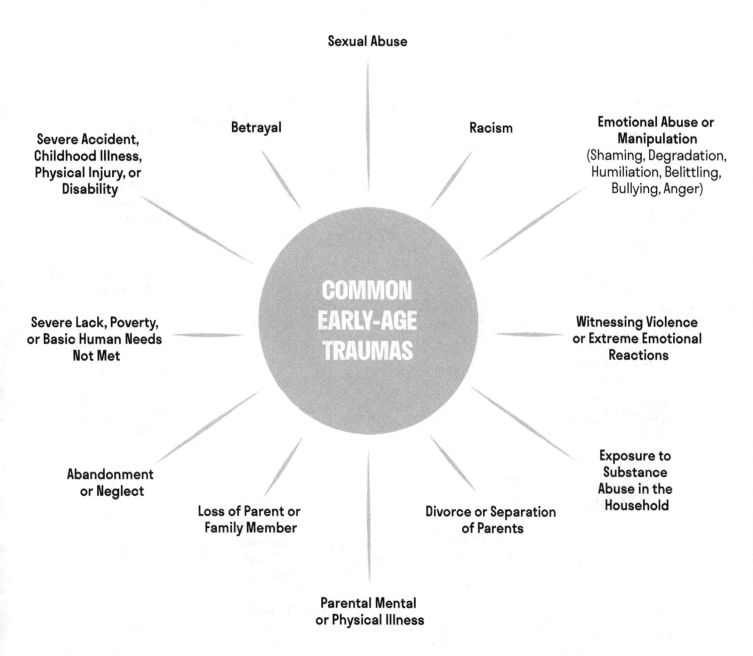

Sexual Abuse

Betrayal

Racism

Emotional Abuse or Manipulation
(Shaming, Degradation, Humiliation, Belittling, Bullying, Anger)

Severe Accident, Childhood Illness, Physical Injury, or Disability

COMMON EARLY-AGE TRAUMAS

Severe Lack, Poverty, or Basic Human Needs Not Met

Witnessing Violence or Extreme Emotional Reactions

Abandonment or Neglect

Exposure to Substance Abuse in the Household

Loss of Parent or Family Member

Divorce or Separation of Parents

Parental Mental or Physical Illness

(Add any you experience by drawing more lines out on the graphic above.)

7

COMMON TRAUMA-INFLUENCED SELF-BELIEFS

"I'm not safe"

"They think I'm stupid"

"I'm going to be rejected"

"I can't have a voice"

"I don't get a choice"

"I need an escape; I need alcohol, drugs, food, etc. to cope"

"I can't love"

"I have little to offer"

"I can't do it"

"I'm going to be betrayed/ tricked"

"I can do no wrong"

"I don't need any help; I'm fine!"

"I'm damaged, 'sinful,' or impure"

"I have to be perfect to be loved"

"It's never my fault"

"I'm going to be punished/ get in trouble"

"It's all my fault"

"I'm a bad person"

"I have many things wrong with me"

"I'm not good enough"

"I can't feel joy"

"Nobody sees me"

"I don't deserve _____"

"It's not fair!"

"I'm breakable"

"I'm alone in the world"

"Nobody loves me"

"I can't make enough money"

"Bad things happen to me"

"I can't commit/ I'll get trapped"

"I'm disgusting"

"I can't have what I want"

"I can't change what happened to me"

"I don't matter; I don't want to be a burden"

(Add any you experience by drawing more lines out on the graphic above.)

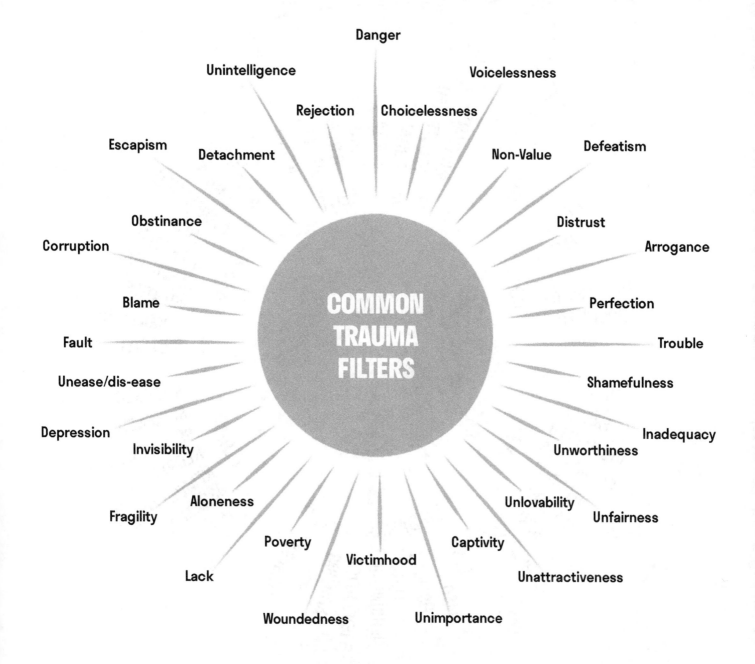

Danger
Unintelligence
Voicelessness
Rejection
Choicelessness
Escapism
Detachment
Non-Value
Defeatism
Obstinance
Distrust
Corruption
Arrogance
Blame
Perfection
Fault
Trouble
Unease/dis-ease
Shamefulness
Depression
Inadequacy
Invisibility
Unworthiness
Aloneness
Unlovability
Fragility
Unfairness
Poverty
Captivity
Lack
Victimhood
Unattractiveness
Woundedness
Unimportance

COMMON TRAUMA FILTERS

(Add any you experience by drawing more lines out on the graphic above.)

COMMON PANEs

RESENTMENT
AVOIDANT
FRUSTRATED
AGITATED
IRRITATED
WRONGED
VENGEFUL
BETRAYED
TRICKED

ANGER
AGGRESSIVE
BURNING
DISRESPECTED
HOSTILE
OFFENDED
RESENTFUL
VOLATILE
HUMILIATED
VIOLATED

SADNESS
ALONE
DESPAIR
HOPELESS
EMPTY
TIRED
DEPRESSED
DISAPPOINTED

GUILT
SHOCKED
SICKENED
SELF-RESENTMENT
REGRET
REMORSEFUL
ASHAMED
EXPOSED
DESPERATE

FEAR
INFERIOR
FRAGILE
VICTIMIZED
POWERLESS
NERVOUS
ANXIOUS
AFRAID
HELPLESS

EMBARRASSMENT
HURT
CONFUSED
FOOLISH
SMALL
DIMINISHED
VULNERABLE
INSECURE
SHAME
REJECTED

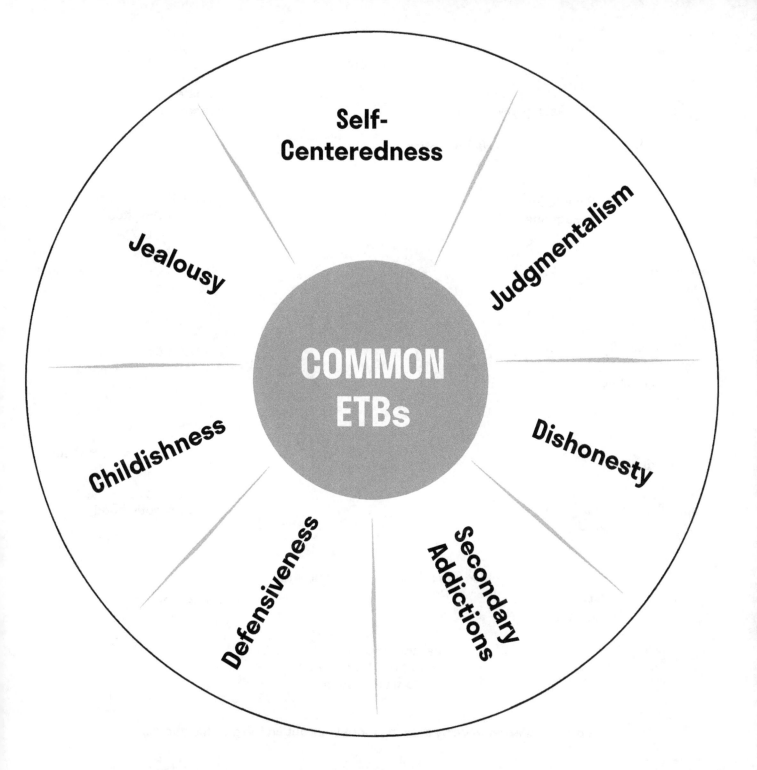

Compete

Get my way

Get attention

Manipulate the outcome

Create distraction

Get info for my agenda

Manage their perception of me or the situation

Prove myself or my worth

Punish them

COMMON MOTIVES

Gain security (financial, prestige, or relational)

Get them to like me / Belong

Be right

Test them

Prove I'm important or loved

Blame / remain in victimhood

Hide something

Control

Not get into trouble

Make them feel what I want them to feel

Make them take action without my direct verbal communication

(Add any you experience by drawing more lines out on the graphic above.)

EMSO FOUNDATIONS

THE *YOU* YOU'VE BEEN BEING

INTRODUCTION TO EMSO FOUNDATIONS: THE *YOU* YOU'VE BEEN BEING

The EMSO Foundations are covered in Chapters 1-25 of the book, "The *You* You've Never Met," and are taught in the first part of the EMSO Essentials online courses. Each Take Action in this journal also appears in the book.

This section allows you to increase awareness of the *you* you've been being in each aspect of emotional insobriety. We'll also look individually at each of the seven common Emotionally-Triggered Behaviors (ETBs) as it applies to your life. This supports you in further clarifying how and where these behaviors show up in your everyday life.

The EMSO Foundations Take Actions aid you in discovering your personal story so that you can clearly identify your own Anatomy of Emotional Insobriety—the most foundational element in beginning your EMSO Training.

I position emotional insobriety as the "seed of life" (depicted on the opposite page) as it gives rise to your eventual Emotional Sobriety. This is important because we must know our starting point—our weak points—which we can then train to become strengths.

Be brave and humble when looking at each component of your emotional insobriety. It's only when we really look at ourselves that we're given an opportunity to change what we no longer desire to keep as part of our identity. If and when this work becomes overwhelming, know that I'm here to guide you and your EMSO Community is here to support you.

EARLY-AGE TRAUMA

TRAUMA-INFLUENCED SELF-BELIEF

INTOXICATED IDENTITY

UNSOBER

TRAUMA FILTER

EMOTIONALLY-TRIGGERED BEHAVIOR (ETB)

BIOCHEMICAL ADDICTION TO PANE

WHY AM I HERE?

Here's your chance to share a "snapshot" of where you are beginning on this journey... something that you'll be able to refer back to at the end and see how far you've come after time passes. You may choose to paste in a current photo.

Write a letter to yourself ("Dear Me Now,"), make a list, and/or create a drawing below to denote your starting point. How do you feel day to day in your life right now? What are your struggles? How do your relationships feel? What situations create resistance in your life? Use the common reasons below as needed.

_____

_____

_____

_____

_____

_____

_____

MOST COMMON REASONS:

- Discord in relationships (abusive or abused)
- Feeling stuck or hopeless
- Feeling of overall dis-ease
- Long-lasting anger, self-pity, helplessness
- Seeming inability to get what you want
- Needing to use things outside of yourself to cope (social media, caffeine, drugs, alcohol, etc.)
- Little ability to stand up for yourself
- Overstepping of others' boundaries
- Lack
- Perpetual negative emotion, depression, anxiety
- Feeling down or unaccomplished
- Feeling easily frustrated; arguing with others in your head
- Often blaming others during discord; feeling victimized
- Relationships that don't serve you or remain in turmoil
- "Giving yourself away" in relationships
- Abusing or controlling others
- The belief that you're right and they're wrong
- Excessive mood swings
- Challenges with children or peers
- A "gap in your game" even if you are successful in other areas
- A feeling that you were meant for something greater

THE REAL ME, PART 1: COMMON TRAITS OF AN EMOTIONALLY SOBER PERSON

As a contrast to where you may be beginning, look at the graphic below. It contains what I commonly see in people who've become emotionally sober. Ask yourself: "Which of these qualities do I wish to attain?" (Yes, it can be all of them!) Circle as many as you wish, and write why you circled these below:

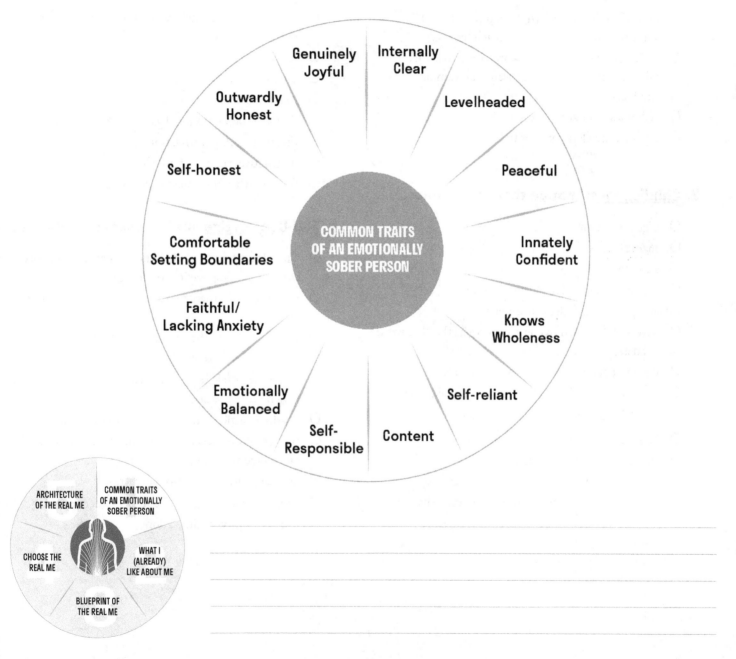

FIND MY ETBs (EMOTIONALLY-TRIGGERED BEHAVIORS)

Are any of the common ETBs part of your <u>current</u> identity? Fill in the circle next to each statement that applies to you.

1. <u>Defensiveness</u>: When threatened, I tend to...

O have a bodily reaction (tighten physically, get a lump in my throat, have stomach tension).

O mentally spin (feel fear or worry, need to justify, talk repetitively or compulsively, question or think obsessively).

O yell or lash out at the messenger.

O cry uncontrollably and/or feel like crying.

2. <u>Childishness</u>: I notice that I sometimes...

O argue to get my way.

O shame others.

O slam doors.

O hit, slap, punch, scratch, and/or bite.

O give people the "silent treatment."

O have a compulsion to control who gets the "last word" in an argument.

O lie to not get in trouble or to get my way.

O throw tantrums (even in public places, making a scene).

O say "It's not fair!" or "It's all your fault!"

O keep harmful secrets (mine or another's).

O am unable to speak (voiceless).

O complain or whine.

O excessively cry or display overly dramatic behavior.

3. <u>Jealousy</u>: I often...

O roll my eyes and "huff" when I notice any attention going away from me.

O cause a scene.

O pick a fight or criticize.

O yell or become aggressive.

O shame or play emotional games.

O threaten ending the relationship.

O destructively compare myself to others.

O feel pain when someone else does well or has what I want.

4. <u>Self-Centeredness</u>: I find that I sometimes...

O think for others (assume I know what someone else is thinking, feeling, saying, or doing).

O overtly direct others to play the roles I want them to in my life.

O passively direct others to get what I want from them.

O have expectations of others (demanded or unspoken).

O interrupt or talk over other people (in argument or in general conversation).

O gossip or slander (as participant or initiator).

O use "emotional leverage" (attempt to impact others' emotional states to get my way).

O get easily offended and/or embarrassed.

O project what I'm "guilty" of onto someone else.

O live in self-pity/victimization.

5. Judgmentalism: I notice that I tend to be...

- O critical of others.
- O critical of myself.
- O avoidant of others who have a different point of view.
- O argumentative when another is not living or thinking as I would.
- O racist, sexist, ageist, etc.
- O judgmental of others for being "guilty of that" as I was reading the above statements.

6. Dishonesty: I notice that I...

- O lie to myself.
- O lie to others (about anything).
- O manipulate others by lying to or about them.
- O am "sneaky."
- O omit select information.

7. Secondary Addiction: I tend to frequently...

use exogenous (external) chemicals, including...

- O drugs (marijuana, cocaine, heroin, pills, etc.).
- O alcohol.
- O nicotine.
- O food.

use distractions, including...

- O phone scrolling, texting, social media.
- O T.V. and streaming (aka "binge" watching).
- O gaming.
- O dating sites.
- O chronically entering into new relationships.
- O mental fantasies (revenge, romantic, sexual, etc.).
- O work/hobbies.
- O trading one addiction for another.

behave compulsively, through...

- O self-injury (cutting, anorexia, bulimia, extreme exercise or diet, etc.).
- O vanity (obsession with appearance; taking daily "selfies," posing/posting for attention, excessive plastic surgery, consumed with looking in mirror, judging body or looks).
- O an inability to be in silence (repetitive chatter, laughing as a defense mechanism, changing topics to deflect, "scatter bomb").
- O isolation/hiding/rebelling.
- O hoarding.
- O spending (shopping, gambling, gift-giving).
- O OCD/repetitive thoughts or actions (body tics or twitches, coughing or sneezing fits, excessive cleaning or hand-washing, turning lights on and off, numerical obsession, etc.).
- O violence (bar fights, street violence, violence for entertainment, gaming).
- O voyeurism/stalking.
- O sex (excessive pornography, affairs, etc.).
- O being restless (not sitting in the same place for long; continuously wanting to move geographically).

BEHAVIORAL AWARENESS

Now that you've made an initial assessment of your possible ETBs, let's practice identifying what specific behaviors you displayed during three recent triggering experiences.

SITUATION 1:

At a time I felt threatened or overwhelmed, this happened:

_____

_____

_____

I reacted by (ETB) _____

_____

_____

SITUATION 2:

At a time I felt threatened or overwhelmed, this happened:

_____

_____

_____

I reacted by (ETB) _____

_____

_____

SITUATION 3:

At a time I felt threatened or overwhelmed, this happened:

_____

_____

_____

I reacted by (ETB) _____

_____

_____

EMOTIONAL AWARENESS

Use the three situations from the previous Take Action for this exercise.

Let's find the real, underlying emotion that you may have been feeling at the time of these events. For example, was your anger or sadness really embarrassment or fear?

How did this experience really make you feel? How do you feel now when you think of it?

Continuously ask yourself: Is it possible that this isn't the real feeling? Can I look deeper?

Refer to the PANE graphic on page 10 to support you in identifying the specific emotion.

Remember the common emotions in EMSO Training are:

R = Resentment

A = Anger

G = Guilt

E = Embarrassment

F = Fear

S = Sadness

SITUATION 1:

During this situation, I used this behavior (ETB):

because I was experiencing the emotion (PANE) of:

SITUATION 2:

During this situation, I used this behavior (ETB):

because I was experiencing the emotion (PANE) of:

SITUATION 3:

During this situation, I used this behavior (ETB):

because I was experiencing the emotion (PANE) of:

BELIEF AWARENESS

Let's find out why this situation triggered you by looking for the Trauma-Influenced Self-Belief that it "validated."

An ETB is brought on by a PANE, and you feel this PANE because you interpret a situation to mean something about you.

By answering this same question again and again, your true self-belief may be revealed.

Refer to the graphic at the beginning of this section to support you in identifying the specific Trauma-Influenced Self-Belief.

SITUATION 1:

What did I interpret the situation to mean about me? _____

_____.

And if this were true, what would <u>that</u> mean about me? _____

_____.

And if that were true, what would <u>that</u> mean about me? _____

_____.

SITUATION 2:

What did I interpret the situation to mean about me? _____

_____.

And if this were true, what would <u>that</u> mean about me? _____

_____.

And if that were true, what would <u>that</u> mean about me? _____

_____.

SITUATION 3:

What did I interpret the situation to mean about me? _____

_____.

And if this were true, what would <u>that</u> mean about me? _____

_____.

And if that were true, what would <u>that</u> mean about me? _____

_____.

MOTIVE AWARENESS

Become a detective and trace the thoughts you were thinking (your internal conversation with yourself) around the time of the behavior.

- What was the real motive behind this behavior?

- What were you hoping to accomplish?

Use the graphic on page 12 to assist you.

EXAMPLES

- "I told him I was going to the movies because I knew he wouldn't attempt to call me during those hours and I could be with the other guy."

- "I said I needed to go buy toilet paper but (underneath) I knew I was really going to buy beer."

- "I mentioned that I was single so that they would overhear and know I was available."

SITUATION 1:

I know I behaved by being (ETB) _____.

I did so specifically by _____.

This seemingly solved my problem by _____

_____.

When I really think about what I was hoping to accomplish by doing this, I know my real motive was to _____

_____.

SITUATION 2:

I know I behaved by being (ETB) _____.

I did so specifically by _____.

This seemingly solved my problem by _____

_____.

When I really think about what I was hoping to accomplish by doing this, I know my real motive was to _____

_____.

SITUATION 3:

I know I behaved by being (ETB) _____.

I did so specifically by _____.

This seemingly solved my problem by _____

_____.

When I really think about what I was hoping to accomplish by doing this, I know my real motive was to _____

_____.

REASONS FOR MY ETBs

After finding which ETBs you demonstrate, look to see the reasons why you specifically may be behaving in these ways.

As you read each of the statements, mark the squares next to those that sound the most like you when you demonstrate that ETB.

Fill in all that apply.

1. <u>Defensiveness:</u>

When I have a bodily reaction (tighten physically, get a lump in my throat, have stomach tension), it's because...

- ☐ I'm guarding by building "a fence"—others can't enter and I can't get out.
- ☐ I feel the need to block my truth from being spoken.
- ☐ I feel fear of speaking up.
- ☐ I think that "I can't speak my truth because I don't know the truth," or because "I won't look perfect by being forthcoming."

When I mentally spin (Ifeel fear or worry, need to justify, talk repetitively or compusively, question or think obsessively), it's because...

- ☐ I feel fear of being rejected, not being loved, or "not being picked for the team."
- ☐ I'm emotionally dependent on the criticizer to like/love me.
- ☐ I assume that if I'm not seen as perfect, I'm not lovable.
- ☐ I'm worried about others.
- ☐ I assume that the worst-case possibilities are an absolute reality.

When I yell or lash out at the messenger, it's because...

- ☐ I have an "I don't like you if you don't like me" attitude.
- ☐ I'm angry at myself for not being perfect or for getting caught.
- ☐ I'm angry with others for not protecting my illusion of perfection.
- ☐ I feel frustrated not knowing how to communicate, or I'm too tired to fix it.
- ☐ I need to reject them before they reject me.

When I cry uncontrollably and/or feel like crying, it's because...

- ☐ I'm being rejected and I'm alone, tired, and exhausted due to not being able to achieve perfection.
- ☐ I feel hopeless and/or helpless.
- ☐ I'm attempting to get what I want; get attention.
- ☐ I'm attempting to create sympathy from another instead of receiving their punishment.
- ☐ I fear not being seen as perfect or not being loved.

2. Childishness:

When arguing to get my way, it's because...

- [ ] I'm committed to a certain emotional state and opinion, and I'm determined to change the other person's stance.
- [ ] I'm holding a motive to win or be right.
- [ ] I'm attempting to control someone else and get what I want.
- [ ] I'm outraged when there's contrast in what I want or believe should be.

When I'm shaming others, it's because...

- [ ] I've brought my experience of shame as a child into adulthood.
- [ ] I want them to feel the same way I think that they made me feel.
- [ ] I feel shame myself but can't name it as such, so I shame others to match my unspoken shame.
- [ ] I have the perception of being on "higher ground" /being more powerful than others.

When I slam doors, it's because...

- [ ] I'm "shutting the other out."
- [ ] I want to manipulate others emotionally.
- [ ] I have feelings—without voicing directly—"I'm angry and feel hopeless in this argument. I may not want to be alone, but I can't be with you."
- [ ] I'm noisily letting others know that they're wrong, in trouble, or being punished.

When I hit, slap, punch, scratch, or bite, it's because...

- [ ] I'm attempting to "tear someone out of their own skin" so they'll see my side.
- [ ] I'm unable to communicate.
- [ ] I want to feel "power over" another person.
- [ ] I don't know what else to do with my frustration.

When I'm giving someone the "silent treatment," I'm really thinking...

- [ ] "If I ignore you, you may see what you're missing."
- [ ] "You may worry about me instead of being angry with me."
- [ ] "Perhaps my withholding of love will make my point and create desperation in you."
- [ ] "If I'm quiet, you'll think of how you've wronged me, and I'll think of how you wronged me too."
- [ ] "My feelings are more important than yours."
- [ ] "I'll build a stronger argument in my head to 'win' the next time we talk."
- [ ] "I need no self-examination nor do I seek responsibility for the conflict."

I have a compulsion to control who gets the "last word" in an argument because...

- [ ] I believe that if the other party has nothing further to say, that means I win the argument ("the defense rests" attitude).
- [ ] I don't seek resolution or connection through conversation.

I lie to not get in trouble or to get my way because...

- [ ] if I tell another this untruth about me, they'll see me the way I desire them to see me, and I'll have perceived control over the situation.
- [ ] I don't want to be punished for what I think I did wrong, or what I believe others will think is wrong.
- [ ] I don't want what's here (reality) to be true.
- [ ] I want to get out of something or to become more likable.
- [ ] I want to blame others for my own discrepancies.
- [ ] I feel threatened and afraid of loss, so I have no choice other than to manipulate others to get the outcome that I want.

...continued

When I throw tantrums (even in public places, making a scene) it's because...

- ☐ I'm "screaming for attention."
- ☐ I want to divert attention away from the truth.
- ☐ I'll do anything to keep the status quo.
- ☐ I can't have a mature conversation.
- ☐ I don't know how else to be seen or heard.

I say, "It's not fair!" or "It's all your fault!" because...

- ☐ I'm struggling to maintain control.
- ☐ I believe I should get my way, or I deserve to get my way.
- ☐ I'm assuming my needs should come first, but I don't voice my precise needs.
- ☐ I'm neglecting to remove myself from chronically imbalanced situations.
- ☐ I have expectations of others.

I keep harmful secrets (mine or another's) because...

- ☐ I'm avoiding "getting in trouble" or protecting someone else from getting in trouble (usually someone with power over me).
- ☐ I can't freely share my harmful or embarrassing experiences with others.
- ☐ I'm protecting myself or others or protecting an image of a desired reality.

I'm unable to speak (voiceless) because...

- ☐ I'm afraid of what might happen if I speak and can't protect myself.
- ☐ I don't believe in myself.
- ☐ I don't know how to use an honest voice in certain situations.

- ☐ I think "I don't have the right to have a voice."
- ☐ I'm unable to communicate well.

I complain or whine because...

- ☐ I'm attempting to make others feel small.
- ☐ I'm relaying information of discomfort or dissatisfaction in the best way I know how.
- ☐ it helps me get attention.
- ☐ I don't know how to fix my troubles or surrounding environment to work better.

I excessively cry or display overly dramatic behaviors because...

- ☐ I want to create distractions so the truth isn't seen.
- ☐ someone may "rescue" me.
- ☐ I often feel confusion with a flood of emotions and it needs to come out.
- ☐ I fear not being seen as perfect, not being loved, or not getting my perceived needs met.
- ☐ I feel hopeless in the moment.

3. Jealousy:

I roll my eyes and "huff" when I notice any attention going away from me because...

- ☐ I'm paranoid of being unimportant or abandoned.
- ☐ I want others to see me and give me attention.
- ☐ I want to be the most special to others.
- ☐ I believe I'm being rejected and I'm resentful.

I cause a scene because...

- ☐ I'm fearful whenever others seem to be out of my personal control.
- ☐ I want to create a big statement so others will chase me.

- ☐ I have the thought, "I'll abandon you if you're going to abandon me."
- ☐ I have to test others to see if they'll choose me.

I pick a fight or criticize because...

- ☐ I fear losing a relationship because of my own inadequacy/insecurity.
- ☐ at least I'll get the other party to feel something for me.
- ☐ I want "connection."
- ☐ now the other person's attention has to be on me.

I yell or become aggressive because...

- ☐ at that moment, I'm certain the other person will choose someone else over me.
- ☐ I've convinced myself that someone else is better than me.
- ☐ I want them to hurt like they hurt me.

I shame or play emotional games because...

- ☐ I want the other to believe that I have the power in the relationship and that I'm the "catch."
- ☐ I want the other to feel small.

I threaten to end the relationship because...

- ☐ I want the other person to fear losing me, as it allows me to regain control.
- ☐ it keeps me at the center of their attention by creating the threat of a "take away."

I destructively compare myself to others because...

- ☐ I'm feeling unaccomplished and insecure.
- ☐ I'm looking to be self-destructive (internally) or gain compliments (externally).
- ☐ I'm keeping myself separate from others.

- ☐ I believe I'm usually in competition with others.
- ☐ I believe that I'm less worthy than others.

I feel pain when someone else does well or has what I want because...

- ☐ I want to be the best at everything.
- ☐ I want myself to be the center of attention when others are receiving praise and respect.
- ☐ I often want what someone else has and am dissatisfied with what I have now.
- ☐ I have an attitude of: "Why do they get that and I don't?"
- ☐ I'm entitled and believe that I deserve something more than another person.
- ☐ I believe others are more likely to withhold things from me rather than share them.

4. Self-Centeredness:

I think for others (assume I know what someone else is thinking, feeling, saying, or doing) because...

- ☐ it helps me manipulate situations and people to stay in control.
- ☐ I assume others can't speak or think for themselves.
- ☐ I'm afraid of what they might be thinking and I need to be ready for what they're about to say or do.

I overtly direct others or assign the roles they'll play in my life because...

- ☐ I believe that others are here to be in my movie of life.
- ☐ I want others to behave the way that I want them to behave.
- ☐ I don't want any changes to the "script."
- ☐ I'm guarding and protecting my autonomy— "This is my life, not yours!"

...continued

I passively direct others to get what I want from them because...

- ☐ it allows me to set up a false stage of my life and get what I want.
- ☐ I want to come out "on top" or be in control in relationships.
- ☐ I'm seeking information for evidence under the guise of sincere interest—to "win" my case.
- ☐ I think, "It doesn't matter how this affects or affected you; all that matters is how I feel and what's happening in me."
- ☐ I can't see clearly outside of myself, and I'm the only thing that's real in my world.

I have expectations of others (demanded or unspoken) because...

- ☐ of my own past experiences or social brainwashings.
- ☐ I think, "I did this for you, so you should've done that for me!"
- ☐ I obsess about how things affect me and I don't realize that others aren't also thinking about how things affect me.

I interrupt or talk over others (in argument or general conversation) because...

- ☐ I've been ignored a lot in the past.
- ☐ I feel impatient or irritable with others' input as I believe I already know what they're going to say and they're wrong.
- ☐ I want to "rule the roost."
- ☐ I'm constantly wondering how I appear to others so I need to make an impression.
- ☐ of the repetitive hysterical thinking in my head.
- ☐ I want others to know I'm important.

I use gossip or slander (as the participant or initiator) because...

- ☐ this form of chaos distracts from my own life.
- ☐ it allows me to get attention.
- ☐ I can hide behind a "veil" of chatter.
- ☐ I can keep my own secrets by telling others' secrets, whether real or false.
- ☐ I can connect with others around shared complaints.
- ☐ by engaging in "mutual enemy relationships" (those built around a mutual enemy or group of adversaries), I feel a sense of belonging and increased power.
- ☐ I perceive that I've been rejected or am feeling shame for something I've done.
- ☐ I take embarrassment and turn it into anger while directing the blame or negative attention "over there."
- ☐ the more people I can get on my side the safer I'll be.
- ☐ I can't contain what I believe happened to me.
- ☐ I want my interpretation of others to be heard.

I use emotional leverage (attempt to impact others' emotional states to get my way) because...

- ☐ it allows me to generate power over someone.
- ☐ I want to be seen as indispensable to another person.
- ☐ if I show my self-sacrifice, others won't leave me.
- ☐ by using shame or guilt, it increases my ability to maintain a relationship.
- ☐ I easily hold onto anger and blame.

I get offended or embarrass easily because...

- ☐ I believe everyone is watching me or talking about me.
- ☐ I chronically analyze others and situations.
- ☐ I'm insecure.

- ☐ I feel entitled to my way even if another person doesn't agree.
- ☐ I see my way as the only way.
- ☐ I'm fairly close-minded in general.
- ☐ I don't often enjoy listening to another's point of view.
- ☐ I think I need to be right.
- ☐ situations are filtered through my thoughts: "What does this have to do with me?" or "What are they thinking of me?" or "Everyone here is as preoccupied with me as I am."

I project what I'm "guilty" of onto others because...

- ☐ I often think, "They're doing this to me!" (not me to them).
- ☐ it's the only thing I can see and declare in others because it's the only thing I experience in myself.

I'm in self-pity/victimization because...

- ☐ I'm establishing myself as someone who needs care, attention, and/or protection.
- ☐ I'm establishing a low baseline—I'm never the one who will be asked for favors; taking the pressure off to contribute/give—"They can't ask me for anything because I'm too _____."
- ☐ I put others on a pedestal; someone else is my hero.
- ☐ I can remain helpless to avoid being perceived as arrogant.
- ☐ it allows soothing compliments to come my way.
- ☐ I'm seeking attention.

5. Judgmentalism:

HINT: A judgment will always have a negative feeling associated with it, whereas an observation won't.

I'm critical of others because...

- ☐ I believe others should live the way I do.
- ☐ others don't fit my paradigm of good or right— e.g., I resent my child for not sharing my religious beliefs (Exclusionary Criticism).
- ☐ I think I'll feel safe if I "control" my surroundings by continuously and disrespectfully pointing out flaws in the environment—e.g., "Don't put that there!" or "Why did you do that?" or "Don't stand like that!" (Vacuum Criticism).
- ☐ I can draw attention away from myself using loud volume so that others' flaws will be seen instead of my own—e.g., "Are you really going to wear that?" or "Why is your floor so dirty?" or "I can't believe you did that!" (Loud Criticism).
- ☐ it validates my perceived power over them.
- ☐ I judge others in the same ways I judge myself.

I'm critical of myself because...

- ☐ I believe I'm lazy.
- ☐ I believe I'm unlovable, uninteresting, or unimportant.
- ☐ I won't ever have to be disappointed if I fail.
- ☐ if I hate myself more than everyone else, no one can reject me.
- ☐ I can get compliments from others if I criticize myself out loud.
- ☐ I think there's no need to try if it's not going to be "perfect."

I'm avoidant of others who have a different point of view because...

- ☐ I don't want to question my upbringing.
- ☐ I don't want to believe or acknowledge that there's an alternative point of view to my own.
- ☐ I believe my opinion is not opinion, but <u>fact</u>.
- ☐ I don't want others to question the way I do things.

...continued

I'm argumentative when another is not living or thinking as I would because...

- [ ] I'm certain of the way things are.
- [ ] I have a right to decide if someone else's life choices are good/bad or right/wrong.
- [ ] there's an alternative point of view than my own.
- [ ] I believe my opinion is not opinion, but <u>fact</u>.
- [ ] I don't want others to question the way I do things.

I'm argumentative when another is not living or thinking as I would because...

- [ ] I'm certain of the way things are.
- [ ] I have a right to decide if someone else's life. choices are good/bad or right/wrong.
- [ ] I have little to no consideration of another's point of view.
- [ ] changing my current lifestyle would be too vulnerable and scary; I perceive I'll have no foundation.

I'm racist/sexist/ageist, etc., because...

- [ ] I feel excessive doubt (especially in my belief system).
- [ ] I've spent my whole life believing what I've believed.
- [ ] I had a difficult experience and now blame the entire group.
- [ ] I was told to be and never changed it (e.g., I may be angered by homosexuality because my parent was vehemently against it).

I was judgmental of others for being "guilty of that" as I was reading the above statements because...

- [ ] it seems easier to put my focus on others before looking at myself and my patterns.
- [ ] I need to observe and criticize others to feel better about myself.

6. <u>Dishonesty:</u>

I lie to myself because...

- [ ] I don't like reality and want to convince myself of an alternative "reality."
- [ ] I don't like who I am or what I'm doing.
- [ ] I want to do something that I think is wrong, so I justify my actions with excuses.

I lie to others (about anything) because...

- [ ] deep down I'm feeling insecure or nervous.
- [ ] I want to be seen a certain way; have a perfect image
- [ ] I'm ashamed or embarrassed.
- [ ] I want the lie to be the truth.

I manipulate others by lying to or about them because...

- [ ] I've decided that they don't deserve the truth.
- [ ] I believe that I know better than they do.
- [ ] it makes my stories more interesting.
- [ ] it makes the context fit my agenda/needs.

I'm sneaky because...

- [ ] I want to have my autonomy, and I believe I'm being controlled.
- [ ] I don't want anyone to know.
- [ ] this is the only thing I have for myself.
- [ ] I feel shame about what I'm doing.

I omit select information because...

- [ ] I don't want to offer information that may poorly affect my desired outcome.
- [ ] if I'm ever found out, I can claim "forgetfulness."
- [ ] I want to shape a conversation to go my way.
- [ ] I've convinced myself that I'm technically still telling the truth if I tell some of it.

7. Secondary Addiction:

I use drugs (marijuana, cocaine, heroin, pills, etc.) because...

- ☐ I need to fill a void in me.
- ☐ I need an immediate change in my reality.
- ☐ it disconnects me from my pain or the mundane.

I drink alcohol because...

- ☐ I need to "fill a void" in me.
- ☐ I'm looking to feel something other than what I'm feeling.
- ☐ I need to "check out" or need "forced" relaxation.
- ☐ I believe I can't have fun without it.
- ☐ I'm shy unless I have it.
- ☐ I believe I'm a better person when I do it.
- ☐ it's in my lineage.

I use nicotine because...

- ☐ everyone in my family and/or circle of friends does it.
- ☐ it calms me down.
- ☐ it keeps me from eating.
- ☐ I've done it since I was a kid.

I eat food addictively because...

- ☐ I need to fill a void in me.
- ☐ I want to numb my emotions.
- ☐ I was deprived of this at some point in my life.
- ☐ I'm "starving" for something.

I distract myself using my phone/scrolling/texting/social media because...

- ☐ I can't be alone.
- ☐ I want to see what everyone else has.
- ☐ it keeps me away from reality.
- ☐ I can live in a fantasy or live vicariously.

I escape by watching T.V./streaming ("binge" watching) because...

- ☐ I want my life to be like what I see on T.V./movies.
- ☐ I get caught up in the drama/romance/violence that I'm watching.
- ☐ it allows me to not have to communicate.
- ☐ I'm alone and it keeps me company.

I escape by gaming because...

- ☐ I like to be in control.
- ☐ I don't know how or who to be in real life.
- ☐ I can drown out my real life.
- ☐ I believe I'm weak, and this makes me feel tough.

I escape by going on dating sites because...

- ☐ I get hits of attention and compliments.
- ☐ I like the excitement of getting attention from a new person.
- ☐ I don't have to commit, but am still "dating."

I escape by chronically entering into new relationships because...

- ☐ I need the rush of something new.
- ☐ I keep thinking, "The next one will be different."
- ☐ I'm chronically looking for "the one."
- ☐ all of my exes were bad for me.
- ☐ I'm dissatisfied with my life and the "grass is always greener on the other side."
- ☐ I can't be alone.

I escape into mental fantasies (revenge, romantic, sexual, etc.) because...

- ☐ I like the gravity of the violence, sex, or emotions.
- ☐ I'm easily bored.
- ☐ I want to continue my same mental obsession I've had since I was young (e.g., fairytale endings).

...continued

I distract myself with work/hobbies because...

- ☐ I'm hiding from intimacy.
- ☐ I believe it's the only way that I add value.
- ☐ I can't show up anywhere else in life.
- ☐ I'm obsessed with what I do.

I distract myself by trading one addiction for another because...

- ☐ I don't want to miss out.
- ☐ I'm bored without some type of addiction.
- ☐ I think that I need something to cope—"at least this is 'healthier.'"

I behave compulsively through self-injury because...

(e.g., cutting, anorexia, bulimia, extreme exercise or diet, etc.)

- ☐ I'm restless/impatient.
- ☐ I can't finish it all or I'm overloaded.
- ☐ I have to perfect my imperfections.
- ☐ pain "wakes me up."
- ☐ I believe I'm ugly/disgusting.
- ☐ I have to look like others think I should look.
- ☐ I can't enjoy food and look good at the same time.
- ☐ I have no value unless I look perfect.
- ☐ I believe I'm too fat or too skinny.

I behave compulsively through vanity because...

(e.g., obsession with appearance; taking daily "selfies," posing/posting for attention, excessive plastic surgery, consumed with looking in the mirror, judging my body or looks)

- ☐ I'm not going to be loved unless I'm attractive.
- ☐ my body has to be precise.
- ☐ I want/receive a lot of attention.
- ☐ no matter what, I can never look good enough.

I behave compulsively with an inability to be in silence because...

(e.g., repetitive chatter, laughing as a defense mechanism, changing topics to deflect, "scatter bomb")

- ☐ I don't know how to simply be myself.
- ☐ I need the attention to both be on and off of me at the same time.
- ☐ in the silence, someone might have an opportunity to ask me a question or say something that makes me uncomfortable.

I behave compulsively by isolating, hiding, or rebelling because...

- ☐ I think I need my autonomy and can't get it.
- ☐ I don't want to be observed, judged, or questioned.
- ☐ I don't want to be controlled.
- ☐ I'm afraid of confrontation.
- ☐ I don't want to be seen or have my secrets revealed.
- ☐ life outside is too overwhelming.
- ☐ I like to dwell on things (fantasize, contemplate, or marinate in my current emotional state).
- ☐ I want to be free from captivity.

I behave compulsively by hoarding because...

- ☐ I'm afraid I'll have nothing if I let things go.
- ☐ I believe that the things I'm keeping might be worth something someday.
- ☐ physical objects keep me safe.
- ☐ I'm never alone when my house is "full."
- ☐ I fear living in lack or poverty.

I behave compulsively through spending (shopping, gambling, gift-giving) because...

- ☐ I want to have everything!
- ☐ I believe if I buy others something they'll like me.

I behave compulsively with OCD/repetitive thoughts or actions because...

(e.g., body tics or twitches, coughing or sneezing fits, excessive cleaning or hand-washing, turning lights on and off, numerical obsession)

- ☐ I don't want to be seen.
- ☐ I need to be seen.
- ☐ I have emotions that I'm shoving down that are trying to come out.
- ☐ it's not safe enough to relax.

I behave compulsively by engaging in violence because...

(e.g., bar fights, street violence, violence for entertainment/gaming)

- ☐ my anger has to go somewhere.
- ☐ I can prove how tough I am/"hard to kill."
- ☐ I can establish myself as not being someone to "mess with."
- ☐ I'm safe if others fear me.

I behave compulsively through voyeurism or stalking because...

- ☐ I become obsessed with people.
- ☐ I need to know what someone is doing at all times.
- ☐ I fear loss and being alone.
- ☐ I don't have an ability to truly connect.
- ☐ if I'm always there, I won't be forgotten.

I behave compulsively through sex (excessive pornography, affairs, etc.) because...

- ☐ it's the only way I can feel anything.
- ☐ I need to know what it would be like.
- ☐ I lack ability for intimacy.

I behave compulsively by being restless because...

(e.g., not sitting in the same place for long, continuously wanting to move geographically)

- ☐ I'm "running away."
- ☐ I'm afraid to stay in one place.
- ☐ the longer I'm still, the more I have to think about my reality.
- ☐ I need to find someone to protect me.
- ☐ I'm anxious that I'll make the wrong choice.
- ☐ I've never had a choice.
- ☐ I'm confused about how I feel and what I want.

Are there any additional reasons for your unwanted behaviors?

_____

_____

_____

_____

_____

_____

_____

_____

_____

_____

LINK THE DETAILS OF MY EMOTIONAL INSOBRIETY

Here's another method we use to find your Trauma-Influenced Self-Beliefs, which is the piece of your anatomy that, when discovered, creates the biggest opportunity for change. These beliefs cause our PANEs, which cause us to re-act using ETBs.

On the examples provided, circle or highlight the Early-Age Traumas that most closely resemble your personal experience.

Then circle the subsequent beliefs, filters, and behaviors that you developed because of it. Use the blank chart at the end for additional. Remember that these were smart strategies that served you well as a child, yet now are only holding you back.

TRAUMA: SEXUAL ABUSE / MOLESTATION

Self-Beliefs	Filters	ETBs
"I'm unworthy"	Unworthiness	Defensiveness
"I'm unsafe"	Danger	Childishness
"I'll be betrayed"	Betrayal	Jealousy
"I'm disgusting"	Unattractiveness	Self-Centeredness
"I'm sick"	Distrust	Judgmentalism
"I'm only valuable sexually"	Non-Value	Dishonesty
"I can't trust"	Victimhood	Secondary Addiction
"I'm a bad person"	Unimportance	
	Voicelessness	
	Choicelessness	

TRAUMA: RACISM, SEXISM

Self-Beliefs	Filters	ETBs
"I'm unworthy"	Unworthiness	Defensiveness
"I'm unsafe"	Lack	Childishness
"I'm disgusting"	Danger	Jealousy
"I'm hated"	Unattractiveness	Self-Centeredness
"I hate _____"	Rejection	Judgmentalism
"I'm a victim"	Non-Value	Dishonesty
"Everyone hates me"	Victimhood	Secondary Addiction
"I'll never make it due to my sex/race"	Unimportance	
	Blame	

TRAUMA: EXPOSURE TO SUBSTANCE ABUSE IN HOUSEHOLD

Self-Beliefs	Filters	ETBs
"I'm going to be just like _____"	Inadequacy	Defensiveness
"I'm not as important as their drugs/alcohol"	Danger	Childishness
"I need drugs/alcohol to cope with my life"	Distrust	Jealousy
"I can't trust anyone"	Rejection	Self-Centeredness
"I'm worthless"	Non-Value	Judgmentalism
"I'll never amount to anything"	Unimportance	Dishonesty
"I have to help others"	Unworthiness	Secondary Addiction
"I have no choice"		

TRAUMA: EMOTIONAL ABUSE

Self-Beliefs	Filters	ETBs
"I'm undeserving"	Unlovability	Defensiveness
"I'm not smart"	Woundedness	Childishness
"I'm unlovable"	Unattractiveness	Jealousy
"I'm not good enough"	Non-Value	Self-Centeredness
"I can't _____"	Voicelessness	Judgmentalism
"I'm a bad person"	Choicelessness	Dishonesty
"I don't have a voice"	Distrust	Secondary Addiction
"I don't get a choice"	Shamefulness	
	Rejection	
	Defeatism	

TRAUMA: VIOLENCE OR WITNESS OF EXTREME EMOTIONAL REACTIONS

Self-Beliefs	Filters	ETBs
"I'm not safe"	Inadequacy	Defensiveness
"I can't trust"	Unworthiness	Childishness
"I have to be loud to be heard"	Danger	Jealousy
"I have t o be silent or I'll get hurt"	Fragility	Self-Centeredness
"I need to control my environment or I'm going to get hurt"	Defeatism	Judgmentalism
	Rejection	Dishonesty
	Victimhood	Secondary Addiction
"I have to be perfect"	Perfection	
	Escapism	
	Captivity	

TRAUMA: LOSS

Self-Beliefs	Filters	ETBs
"Everyone leaves me"	Obstinance	Defensiveness
"If I feel nothing, I'll be safer"	Detachment	Childishness
"I'm often sick like the one I lost"	Unworthiness	Jealousy
"If I appear perfect no one will leave me"	Danger	Self-Centeredness
"I can't trust"	Fragility	Judgmentalism
	Defeatism	Dishonesty
	Rejection	Secondary Addiction
	Victimhood	
	Perfection	
	Lack	
	Distrust	

TRAUMA: LACK OR POVERTY

Self-Beliefs	Filters	ETBs
"I never have enough"	Lack	Defensiveness
"I can't get my needs met"	Poverty	Childishness
"I'm not the kind of person who can have it all"	Unimportance	Jealousy
	Unworthiness	Self-Centeredness
"If I were loved (by others or God), I'd have more"	Inadequacy	Judgmentalism
	Defeatism	Dishonesty
"People who are rich are evil"	Victimhood	Secondary Addiction
	Danger	
"I don't want to be like rich people"	Escapism	
	Shamefulness	
"If I had more, I'd be worth more to others"	Non-Value	
	Obstinance	
	Perfection	

TRAUMA: DELIVERED TRAUMA (BY YOU)

Self-Beliefs	Filters	ETBs
"I'm a bad person"	Unworthiness	Defensiveness
"I should be ashamed"	Unease/dis-ease	Childishness
"I'm disgusting"	Danger	Jealousy
"I'm going to get in trouble"	Distrust	Self-Centeredness
"I'm scared of people knowing what I did"	Non-Value	Judgmentalism
	Unattractiveness	Dishonesty
"I don't deserve ___"	Rejection	Secondary Addiction
"It's always my fault"	Shamefulness	
"I can't change"	Trouble	
	Unlovability	
	Perfection	
	Obstinance	

...continued

TRAUMA: <u>ABANDONMENT OR NEGLECT</u>		
Self-Beliefs	Filters	ETBs
"I'm probably going to be left or betrayed"	Unimportance	Defensiveness
"I'm of no value"	Perfection	Childishness
"I'm unworthy of love"	Unworthiness	Jealousy
"I'm inadequate"	Rejection	Self-Centeredness
"Something's wrong with me"	Unlovability	Judgmentalism
"I'm not important"	Victimhood	Dishonesty
"I'll never be loved"	Detachment	Secondary Addiction
"If I'm perfect, I won't be left"	Inadequacy	
"I'm not special"	Shamefulness	
	Escapism	
	Captivity	
	Voicelessness	
	Trouble	
	Distrust	

TRAUMA: <u>DIVORCE OF PARENTS/ SINGLE PARENT</u>		
Self-Beliefs	Filters	ETBs
"I can't trust"	Unimportance	Defensiveness
"If they loved me, they would've stayed together or wouldn't have left me"	Unworthiness	Childishness
	Rejection	Jealousy
	Perfection	Self-Centeredness
	Distrust	Judgmentalism
"I'm worthless"	Danger	Dishonesty
"I'm no good"	Inadequacy	Secondary Addiction
"I have to be perfect"	Non-Value	
"It was my fault"	Victimhood	
"I'm unlovable"	Fault	
	Trouble	
	Unlovability	
	Invisibility	
	Detachment	
	Aloneness	

TRAUMA: <u>BETRAYAL</u>		
Self-Beliefs	Filters	ETBs
"I'm unimportant"	Unimportance	Defensiveness
"I'm a joke"	Unworthiness	Childishness
"I'm of no value"	Rejection	Jealousy
"I'm always 'ready' to be betrayed"	Distrust	Self-Centeredness
"I can't trust"	Danger	Judgmentalism
"I'm unsafe"	Inadequacy	Dishonesty
"I'll be tricked again"	Non-Value	Secondary Addiction
"They think I'm stupid"	Victimhood	
	Perfectionism	
	Unintelligence	
	Obstinance	

TRAUMA: _____		
Self-Beliefs	Filters	ETBs

MY TRAUMA PATHWAY

Use the next several pages to work through several of your Early-Age Traumas. If you need additional space, use extra paper to answer these five questions for each experience of trauma. Remember, right now we're looking only at trauma from around ages 0 to 20.

Early-Age Trauma #1: _____

1. What was said or done to you, or what did you observe, perceive, deliver, or have inflicted upon you? _____
   _____
   _____

2. What do you now believe about yourself because of this event? What are your Trauma-Influenced Self-Beliefs? _____
   _____
   _____

3. What Trauma Filters are in place to validate your Trauma-Influenced Self-Beliefs? _____
   _____
   _____

4. When you believe this, how do you feel, both in your physical body and emotionally speaking (PANEs)? _____
   _____
   _____

5. What tendencies do you now have due to this trauma? What are your ETBs? _____
   _____
   _____

Early-Age Trauma #2: _____

1. What was said or done to you, or what did you observe, perceive, deliver, or have inflicted upon you? _____
   _____
   _____
   _____

2. What do you now believe about yourself because of this event? What are your Trauma-Influenced Self-Beliefs? _____
   _____
   _____
   _____

3. What Trauma Filters are in place to validate your Trauma-Influenced Self-Beliefs? _____
   _____
   _____
   _____

4. When you believe this, how do you feel, both in your physical body and emotionally speaking (PANEs)? _____
   _____
   _____
   _____

5. What tendencies do you now have due to this trauma? What are your ETBs? _____
   _____
   _____
   _____

Early-Age Trauma #3:

1. What was said or done to you, or what did you observe, perceive, deliver, or have inflicted upon you?

2. What do you now believe about yourself because of this event? What are your Trauma-Influenced Self-Beliefs?

3. What Trauma Filters are in place to validate your Trauma-Influenced Self-Beliefs?

4. When you believe this, how do you feel, both in your physical body and emotionally speaking (PANEs)?

5. What tendencies do you now have due to this trauma? What are your ETBs?

Early-Age Trauma #4: _____

1. What was said or done to you, or what did you observe, perceive, deliver, or have inflicted upon you? _____
_____
_____
_____

2. What do you now believe about yourself because of this event? What are your Trauma-Influenced Self-Beliefs? _____
_____
_____
_____

3. What Trauma Filters are in place to validate your Trauma-Influenced Self-Beliefs? _____
_____
_____
_____

4. When you believe this, how do you feel, both in your physical body and emotionally speaking (PANEs)? _____
_____
_____
_____

5. What tendencies do you now have due to this trauma? What are your ETBs? _____
_____
_____
_____

Early-Age Trauma #5: _____

1. What was said or done to you, or what did you observe, perceive, deliver, or have inflicted upon you? _____

____

2. What do you now believe about yourself because of this event? What are your Trauma-Influenced Self-Beliefs? ____

____

3. What tendencies do you now have? What Trauma Filters are in place? _____

____

4. When you believe this, how do you feel, both in your physical body and emotionally speaking (PANEs)? ____

____

5. What tendencies do you now have due to this trauma? What are your ETBs? _____

____

SNAPSHOT OF MY ANATOMY OF EMOTIONAL INSOBRIETY

You're now more aware of your Anatomy of Emotional Insobriety. Here's an opportunity to consolidate all that you've learned about yourself into one simple design. Write your most impactful Early-Age Trauma(s), then work your way around clockwise, adding each component to the chart on the opposite page. Consolidate what you've learned about yourself regarding each part of your anatomy into one to three total examples. This will become your reference point to remind you what you learned about the *you* you've been being—your Intoxicated Identity.

EARLY-AGE
TRAUMA

INTOXICATED
IDENTITY

TRAUMA-INFLUENCED
SELF-BELIEF

EMOTIONALLY-TRIGGERED
BEHAVIOR (ETB)

TRAUMA
FILTER

BIOCHEMICAL
ADDICTION
TO PANE

DEFENSIVENESS: OBSERVE MY (DE)FENCES

Read each statement and fill in the circles next to the ones that sound like you when you think you are being threatened or criticized.

Mark all that apply:

O There are secrets I keep for myself or others, and when people pry, I fiercely defend them.

O I feel something come over me and suddenly I'm putting up a "fence" to keep the other person or situation away.

O When people point something out about me, I feel agitated and can't listen.

O When I receive criticism—even if it's constructive—I see the same thing about myself but feel helpless about changing it, and then I get defensive.

O I lie about something surrounding the threatening situation or the other person who's being critical.

O I hide my flaws in an effort to present myself as "perfect" to others.

O I get embarrassed easily. I sense I'm being observed.

O When I feel rejected, instead of saying anything I close down.

O I realize now that it's possible that my defensiveness comes from being emotionally unsober.

O Others: _____

_____

_____

_____

_____

_____

_____

_____

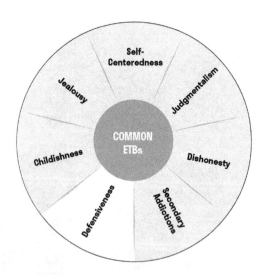

DEFENSIVENESS: REACTING TO NEGATIVE FEEDBACK

PART 1: First, note any challenging behaviors or traits you demonstrate that have been brought to your attention by a friend, family member, co-worker, or partner:

PART 2: Next, you'll need to call or meet with a trusted friend, parent, or romantic partner. Ask this person to either read the list above out loud to you in this way: "You do _____ and you are _____."

Or, they may know you well and be able to share their own feedback without using the list. After they offer this feedback, think about what they shared and respond to these questions:

This is here to help you get a sense of how you respond or react to feedback or perceived criticism.

WARNING: If you're unsure you can remain calm after hearing their feedback, simply imagine them giving you feedback without inviting the meeting, and write about it below.

- How do I feel in my physical body and emotions (PANEs) right now?

- Does their feedback feel true to me? If not, why?

CHILDISHNESS: MY "FIVE-YEAR-OLD" SELF

Read each statement and fill in the circle next to the statement that sounds like you, and take note throughout the next few days when you're expressing childish behavior.

Mark all that apply:

HINT: You may be very surprised to see your resemblance to your "five-year-old" self (in thinking, feeling, and behaving) when you encounter even mildly stressful situations.

O When I cry, I expect people to come to my rescue.

O I believe that if I want something or someone, I should be able to have it or them, whenever I want.

O I've hit or slapped someone in the past, or continue to do this presently.

O When I fear that I might get in trouble, I create little white lies to ensure that others don't catch me.

O If I don't get my way, I make a fuss about it until I do.

O I avoid conflict or uncomfortable situations even if I'm responsible for them.

O I often feel powerless to fix things.

O I don't communicate, even when it's important, in order to "prove a point," gain control, make others upset, or because I'm too scared to have a voice.

O When I'm asked to respond, I often don't know what to say or what the outcome may be, so I hide out and avoid.

O I believe that if I'm expected to communicate, it means I'm being controlled.

O Other childish behaviors you are expressing:

_____

_____

_____

_____

_____

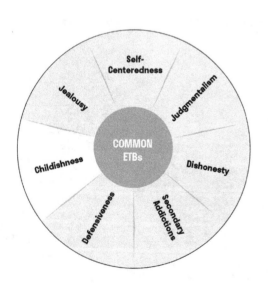

CHILDISHNESS: CHILDHOOD NEEDS

What needs have followed you into adulthood? Look at some examples of childhood needs here and fill in the circle next to the ones that apply to you.

Mark all that apply:

HINT: Think of the needs that might match your Trauma Filters. They'll be most obvious when you can look at where your ETB of Childishness is expressed due to not getting them met.

For example, when do you throw a tantrum? Excessively cry? Believe you've been defeated? Feel shame? Have a sense you're rejected?

I often need to...

O be the most important person in the room.

O have most of others' spare time spent with me.

O have things done for me.

O have everything go my way, or the way I believe it should.

O be right.

O receive gifts on special days.

O receive approval.

O receive verbal validation.

O explain myself, even without others asking.

O be understood, even if it doesn't seem possible that I could explain myself correctly.

O have others make decisions for me.

O Any other childhood needs coming to mind?

_____

_____

_____

_____

_____

_____

ROMANTIC JEALOUSY: FACE MY JEALOUS NATURE

Describe the last experience you had of expressing romantic jealousy to someone in your life using these questions.

- What did you say to the other person(s), or how did you behave?

  _____

  _____

  _____

- What did you feel before you behaved jealously?

  _____

  _____

  _____

- How did they respond?

  _____

  _____

  _____

- What were you thinking about yourself?

  _____

  _____

  _____

- If you'd come from a place of security instead of insecurity, what might you have asked them or done instead?

  _____

  _____

  _____

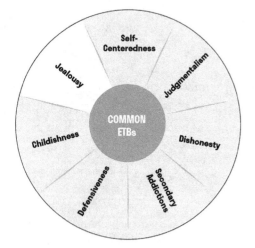

COMPARISON JEALOUSY: CHALLENGE MY TRIGGERS

Think of the last time you were emotionally triggered by a jealous thought toward another person, such as:

- "I want what they have."

- "I want to be like them, and I never will be."

- "They have such a great relationship, and I'll never have that."

- "Why can't I... ?"

Write down the qualities you see in this person or in this person's life:

_____
_____
_____
_____
_____
_____
_____
_____
_____
_____

Now imagine that these qualities are describing you or your life. In what ways are you the same? What's one step you can take to embody one quality from this list?

_____
_____
_____
_____
_____
_____
_____
_____
_____
_____

SELF-CENTEREDNESS: LOOKING CLEARLY AROUND ME

Review your day today. Write down five moments when you were self-centered.

When were you attention-seeking?

When did you easily take offense?

When did you experience concern that others were talking about you or thinking badly of you?

When did you interpret others' actions or words to mean something about you?

If none of this occurred for you today, choose a recent experience where you were self-centered and describe it here:

1. _____

2. _____

3. _____

4. _____

5. _____

SELF-CENTEREDNESS: CENTER OF SELF

Refer to the "House of Mirrors" visualization you completed in "The *You* You've Never Met" or your coursework. Recall that while you were inside your house of mirrors, you likely experienced a variety of thoughts, feelings, and behaviors.

When you imagined being trapped inside that room for the entire day, which of the following occurred? Mark all that apply:

O   I felt afraid and wanted to "make it stop!"

O   I started judging what was right and wrong about myself.

O   I imagined a worst-case scenario.

O   It felt secure... "I know best and don't trust anyone anyway!"

O   I was easily offended.

O   I felt alone and realized I was isolated from everyone.

O   I felt sad.

O   I was quick to anger at various moments.

O   I envied the people outside the room.

O   I felt self-conscious about what others might be seeing.

O   I kept myself distracted by staying busy to avoid feeling.

O   I couldn't give genuine attention to anyone or anything outside of the room.

O   I wanted "payback" from someone.

O   I felt like a victim and blamed someone—"You did this to me!" or "This is your fault!" or "Can't you see me?!"

O   I couldn't be vulnerable or let my guard down.

O   I was irritated.

O   Other: _____

FREEDOM OF SELF

When you explored life <u>outside</u> your House of Mirrors, you likely experienced a different set of thoughts, feelings, and behaviors.

When you imagined being in your beautiful place for the entire day, which of the following occurred? Mark all that apply:

O   I laughed at my "mistakes."

O   I didn't worry about others' "mistakes."

O   I related with others.

O   I felt confident but not cocky.

O   I didn't compare myself to others.

O   I was open to sharing time and space with others—"You can come to me and I can see you clearly," or "My space is your space."

O   I found ways to help others.

O   I felt happy.

O   I wasn't guarded or "needing space."

O   I didn't really have any problems.

O   I shared myself vulnerably.

O   I was relaxed.

O   If I did feel something (fear, sadness, anger, etc.) it didn't last long before I came back to a sense of freedom.

O   Other: _____
      _____
      _____

JUDGMENTALISM: MEET MY INNER CRITIC

Take a moment to review the list of Common Traits of an Emotionally Sober Person (found on page 17) regarding who you want to become.

List those that you circled:

_____

_____

_____

_____

Answer each of these questions about yourself and see if you get to meet the judge within you.

- When you consider the traits you'd like to have, do any inner criticisms come up?

  _____

  _____

- What are your top three "I can't..." stories when you consider adding these traits to your life?

  1 _____

  2 _____

  3 _____

- When do you most often judge yourself? (e.g., you caught yourself judging others 15 times today, so you start judging yourself for judging them!).

  _____

  _____

JUDGMENTALISM: DIFFERENT FROM ME

Think of someone in your life who acts, believes, or thinks differently from you. Then answer these questions:

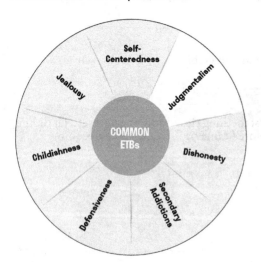

- What do you feel in your body (e.g., tension, numbness, burning, etc.)?

  _____

  _____

- What PANEs (emotions) do you feel?

  _____

  _____

- How do you typically behave (ETBs) around them?

  _____

  _____

JUDGMENTALISM: OBSERVE THE JUDGE

This is an exercise of both self-observation and journaling.

How often are you analyzing others with feelings of resentment, disgust, anger, or even embarrassment on their behalf?

At this point, this exercise is for you to only observe yourself and your habits in thinking and judging—not to share your judgments with the people you're judging.

Share the inner workings of your thought patterns, and you'll begin to look at yourself from different angles.

- Check your inner dialogue and feelings that arise when you witness another living different from how you would. Observe yourself and what you're noticing around your habit of judgment. Share how you feel when you're judging.

  _____

  _____

  _____

- Recognize what you feel when you're judging versus when you're not. How much freer do you feel when you're coming from an open mind versus a judging mind?

  _____

  _____

  _____

- Acknowledge when you've been judged in the past and how that felt. What do you wish the other person would have noticed about your choices? How do you wish they would have responded to you?

  _____

  _____

  _____

DISHONESTY: UNCOVER MY UNCONSCIOUS LIES

For the entire day tomorrow, take this journal with you or use a voice memo or note in your phone and write down each time you lie to someone else, think about lying, or lie to yourself.

Then, respond to these inquiries:

1. How might you presently be wasting someone else's time by telling them what you think they want to hear, rather than the truth?

_____

_____

_____

_____

2. When have you done so in the past?

_____

_____

_____

3. Write about an experience when you were dishonest to make it seem to others that you were more attractive/kind/special:

_____

_____

_____

_____

4. What may you be lying about in order to "not get in trouble"?

_____

_____

_____

_____

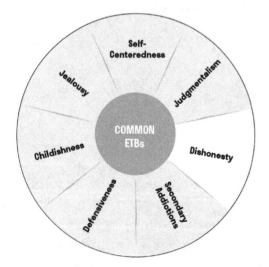

DISHONESTY: REALITY CHECKPOINTS

To grow your honesty muscle, practice asking the following throughout your day tomorrow: What's R.E.A.L. in this moment? (Am I revealing everything accurately in life <u>right now</u>?). To deepen this practice, try pausing three times (perhaps after each meal) and asking yourself these four questions honestly, realistically, and slowly:

	REALITY CHECKPOINTS		
	MORNING	AFTERNOON	EVENING
What's <u>actually</u> existing in this moment? (not imagined)			
What are my <u>genuine</u> feelings? (not the feelings I think I'm supposed to be feeling)			
What am I <u>actually</u> intending? (not what I wish I were intending)			
What's the <u>accuracy</u> of this? (not something I'm making up to fit my agenda)			

SECONDARY ADDICTION: WHAT THEY SAY ABOUT ME

Have others mentioned that you may have an unhealthy addiction (e.g. "You drink too much!" or "Why are you such a loner?" or "Can I help you quit smoking?" or "You're on your phone all the time!"

HINT: These are things that you may do without even knowing you're doing them, but others have tried to bring them to your attention.

List the secondary addictions that others have accused you of having, even if you don't agree:

_____

_____

_____

_____

_____

_____

SECONDARY ADDICTION: THE THOUGHTS IN MY HEAD

These are the things you may think to yourself and/or excuses you make regarding your secondary addiction. Mark all the apply to you:

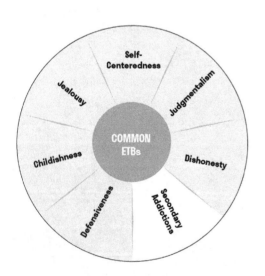

- O Just one more.
- O I need this to fill a void.
- O No one needs to know.
- O I deserve something "bad."
- O I wasn't allowed to have this before; now I want all of it.
- O I need to feel something else.
- O I can't have fun without it.
- O This is the only way I can relax.
- O It's in my lineage.
- O I need this for my pain.
- O I have to do this, or I'll go crazy.
- O I have this under control.
- O I can quit anytime.
- O I don't want to miss out.

SECONDARY ADDICTION: ADMIT TO MYSELF

Review what you wrote on the opposite page and what you know to be true about yourself. Using one or two of your secondary addictions, fill in the following statements.

If you'd like to add more, continue on a separate piece of paper.

Remember, this is only for you. Can you get real with yourself right now? You're not alone, as everyone has experienced or currently experiences at least one secondary addiction.

HINT: I define an "unhealthy amount" as:

- Damaging my body

- Interfering with my self-care

- Disturbing my relationships or work

- Having a negative impact on children

1. When I'm honest with myself, I know that I _____ _____ in an unhealthy amount.

2. I tend to do this in order to _____ _____ .

3. The reason I do this specifically is that it makes me feel _____ _____ .

4. The first time I did this was because _____ _____ .

5. What harm has this caused me or others? ____ _____ _____ _____ .

6. I've been doing this for _____ years.

7. I've tried quitting, but (if applicable) _____ _____ _____ .

8. When I look honestly, I see that I'm addicted to _____ _____ .

CHECK MY MOTIVE

After having explored each of the seven most common ETBs, it's important to begin to develop a new level of maturity before moving on to EMSO Investigations. You can do this by growing the capacity to do what we call in EMSO, "Check Motive." This is one of the foundations of EMSO Training.

Think of the last time you used each of the common ETBs and write in your motive, meaning:

- What was I hoping to accomplish by behaving this way?

- Why did I behave in this way?

Use the graphic on page 12 to assist you.

1. I was defensive so that _____

_____

2. I was childish so that _____

_____

3. I was jealous so that _____

_____

4. I was self-centered so that _____

_____

5. I was judgmental so that _____

_____

6. I was dishonest so that _____

_____

7. I used a secondary addiction so that _____

_____

Additional examples:

_____

_____

_____

SUMMARY OF EMSO FOUNDATIONS: THE *YOU* YOU'VE BEEN BEING

Our Early-Age Trauma usually directs who we become, and with repetition of our cycles of addiction, and being amongst similar personalities, we often don't even realize who we've been being! Remember, we're all the same in that we each have our own form of suffering and compulsive behaviors. Each Take Action you've just completed was here to promote self-awareness, not shame.

Now that you've explored the Anatomy of your Emotional Insobriety, including each ETB in great detail, how has your past made you the *you* you're now being? Can you see more clearly who you became due to your biochemical addiction to PANEs, which is sustained by your Trauma-Influenced Self-Beliefs and Trauma Filters? Do you see your ETBs?

Before moving onto your EMSO INVESTIGATIONS, make sure you've completed the EMSO FOUNDATIONS, and give yourself time to reflect on this section and what you learned about yourself. Free-write and/or draw below.

The EMSO FOUNDATIONS have given you much more <u>awareness</u>, and next you'll move on with <u>acknowledging</u> how they've influenced your life and the lives of those around you...

EMSO INVESTIGATIONS

THE *YOU* YOU'VE NEVER NOTICED

INTRODUCTION TO EMSO INVESTIGATIONS: THE *YOU* YOU'VE NEVER NOTICED

Now that you've completed the EMSO FOUNDATIONS, you begin EMSO INVESTIGATIONS. The bulk of this section includes what I term the "EMSO MASTER CHART." You'll see this symbol each time there's something to add to it:

Take a moment now to turn to the back of this journal to glance at the chart and begin to familiarize yourself with it. This will be used quite a bit throughout your EMSO Training. Use the first blank chart until it's filled in and then move on to the next copy as needed. There are 10 blank copies included. If you need additional copies, download them from your member page: **liftedacademy.com/tyynm**.

*NOTE: It's important that you only complete what the <u>current</u> Take Action asks of you without reading ahead in "The *You* You've Never Met" book and adjunct courses, as the EMSO MASTER CHART is filled out in a particular sequence.

THE REAL ME, PART 2: WHAT I (ALREADY) LIKE ABOUT ME

You deserve a little "exhale" after the challenging topics you've had to face thus far in your EMSO Foundations.

In The Real Me, Part 1 on page 17, you considered which emotionally sober traits you wished to attain in the future. Next, list five (or more) things you like about yourself, what others like about you, or things that you intend to keep as a part of your chosen identity going forward.

1. _____

2. _____

3. _____

4. _____

5. _____

Additional: _____

_____

_____

_____

_____

_____

_____

_____

_____

_____

_____

_____

_____

_____

_____

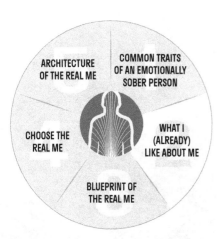

63

MY LIFE MOVIE: STOPPING PLACES

Either read the "My Life Movie" Contemplation in the book and/or go to your free downloads page at liftedacademy.com/tyynm and pull up the recording called "My Life Movie." Close your eyes and "watch your movie." Write the first five stopping places.

HINTS:

- Write down your "first five" right away. Get them out now, as these are your biggest blocks.

- These moments may either be in the distant or recent past, and they usually involve the moments where your actions hurt others or yourself, and/or bring embarrassment, regret, or shame.

- Your stopping places are the ones you wish no one (including you) would ever have to see again.

Take a break, such as a walk or at minimum a few deep breaths and come back later to write down <u>all</u> of your stopping places.

Write these in list form—only a few words for now—enough for you to know what they mean. You'll use this as you continue your investigation.

Where in the film would I like to hit the stop button so no one will ever see what I see? Who did I hurt? What did I do? Or, what happened to me?

1. _____

2. _____

3. _____

4. _____

5. _____

MY LIFE MOVIE: IF EVERYONE REALLY SAW

Fill in the following statement for your first five stops, then as many times as is necessary to further discover any remaining stops in "My Life Movie."

Continue using the PANE graphic on page 65 to help identify the real feeling as needed.

1. I want to hit the stop button when I think about this scene, person, or situation from my past... _____

_____ ,

because if everyone in the "movie theater" saw this, I would feel _____

_____ .

2. I want to hit the stop button when I think about this scene, person, or situation from my past... _____

_____ ,

because if everyone in the "movie theater" saw this, I would feel _____

_____ .

3. I want to hit the stop button when I think about this scene, person, or situation from my past... _____

_____ ,

because if everyone in the "movie theater" saw this, I would feel _____

_____ .

4. I want to hit the stop button when I think about this scene, person, or situation from my past... _____

_____ ,

because if everyone in the "movie theater" saw this, I would feel _____

_____ .

5. I want to hit the stop button when I think about this scene, person, or situation from my past... _____

_____ ,

because if everyone in the "movie theater" saw this, I would feel _____

_____ .

ACKNOWLEDGE WHOM I'VE HURT

Review your stopping places and use these prompts to acknowledge who you've hurt. Did any of your ETBs hurt any of these people in your life?

- Romantic Interests/Partners
- Family Members
- Children
- Friends/Acquaintances
- Co-workers
- Coaches
- Teachers/Mentors
- Strangers

Include yourself on this list, as well as those who have passed away.

Now turn to your first EMSO MASTER CHART. These are the first people to write in Column A: NAMES. Then, add to Column B: SITUATION by writing what happened in your Life Movie with this person.

I lied to:

I cheated on:

I physically hurt:

I bullied:

I emotionally manipulated:

I stole from:

I neglected, disregarded, or used:

I hurt:

BODY SIGNALS

Get out your primary devices (phone, computer, tablet, etc.) and/or address book, and take a moment to slowly look through the names of people in your various contacts lists, inboxes, and friends lists.

As you read each name, pay attention to the changes within your body when you think about that specific person, group, or situation.

Do you feel any strangeness in your body (see list for examples)? This strange feeling indicates an unresolved issue; and that means this NAME must make it onto your EMSO MASTER CHART!

Add them now to Column A: NAMES, and respond to the question in Column B: SITUATION for each.

Here are some things to feel for:

- Boiling sensation from legs to head (overwhelm)

- Shaking or rumbling in your solar plexus

- Acidity

- Fist clenching

- Jaw tension

- Stomach discomfort

- Tightness around the naval, wrapping around rib cage

- Nausea

- Dizziness

- Tingling

- Anxiety

- Nervousness

- Fatigue

- Squeezing of chest

- Lump or tension in throat

- Rectal changes

- Hunching of shoulders (hiding heart center)

- Becoming smaller

- Other: _____

_____

_____

PANES BY AGE

Next, go a little more slowly, and review your life age by age, looking for any PANE that arises when you consider what was happening to you and around you during each of these time periods.

For each of the following ages, recall the individual people, groups, and situations with whom you were angry during that period of life, anyone you continue to harbor resentment toward, and with whom you feel guilty or embarrassed. Explore your fear and sadness during each age range.

Then go to your EMSO MASTER CHART and add each new name from this exercise in a box in the Column A: NAME and share what happened in Column B: SITUATION.

AGE	RESENTMENT I was hurt by:	ANGER I was angry with:	GUILT This person made me feel guilt:	EMBARRASS-MENT This person embar-rassed me:	FEAR I felt fear with:	SADNESS I felt sadness with:
0-5						
6-10						
11-17						
18-21						
22-29						
30-39						
40-59						
60-75						
76+						

INSTITUTIONAL PANES

What are the groups or institutions that you've encountered throughout your life for which you feel resentment, anger, guilt, embarrassment, fear, or sadness?

These might be organizations, institutions, civic groups, schools, etc. If it helps to spark your memory, go age by age again.

HINTS:

- *Review your life experiences with your religion, school, or workplace.*

- *This is also where Observed Traumas are often noted. What situation did you observe that left you with PANEs? This could be something you saw or experienced as a first responder, doctor, parent, counselor, etc.*

Transfer the names of these groups and the situations to Columns A: NAMES and Column B: SITUATION.

I resent:

_____
_____
_____
_____
_____
_____

I'm embarrassed by:

_____
_____
_____
_____
_____
_____

I'm angry with:

_____
_____
_____
_____
_____
_____

I feel fear with:

_____
_____
_____
_____
_____
_____

I feel guilt around:

_____
_____
_____
_____
_____
_____

I feel sadness about:

_____
_____
_____
_____
_____
_____

THE SEX SCENES

With whom have you had either romantic or non-romantic sexual relationships? Where in "My Life Movie" did you hit the STOP button during a sex scene? List them all here, or at the very least, those whom you've hurt or who've hurt you:

HINTS:

- *If it helps prompt your memory, go age by age again.*

- *This is completely confidential between <u>you</u> and <u>you</u> right now. Be specific and thorough.*

- *If shame arises, feel it and write it anyway. If the paper gets wet from your tears as you remember past love or difficulties, dry off the page and continue.*

Add these to Column A: NAMES and what happened in Column B: SITUATION on your EMSO MASTER CHART.

Romantic Sexual Partners:

_____

_____

_____

_____

_____

_____

_____

_____

_____

_____

_____

_____

_____

_____

_____

Non-romantic Sexual Partners:

_____

_____

_____

_____

_____

_____

_____

_____

_____

_____

_____

_____

_____

_____

_____

BELIEF/FILTER

What does this mean about me?

For each row on your EMSO Master Chart, use your developing self-awareness from EMSO Foundations to identify the self-belief that this particular person, group, or situation validates about you.

Fill in Column C: BELIEF/FILTER for each line using the code from the key on page 91 for the appropriate Trauma Filter(s) and/or write out the Trauma-Influenced Self-Belief if that helps you.

This [situation] was difficult because of my Trauma-Influenced Self-Belief(s) of:

_____

_____ .

I may be filtering this person, group, or situation through my Trauma Filter(s) of:

_____

_____ .

PANE

What emotion(s) do I feel because of this self-belief?

This is your chance to uncover what you're truly feeling in relation to each person, group, or situation on your EMSO MASTER CHART. It's important to know what you're feeling—not what you or others <u>think</u> you should be feeling, nor what you wish you were feeling.

Fill in Column D: PANE by circling the letter(s) for the emotion(s) that most closely matches what you feel. If it's not one of the most common six, write in what it is using the graphic on page 90.

HINT: It's common to have more than one PANE/emotion.

Because I've convinced myself that [belief/filter], I now feel:

_____

_____ .

ETB

What behavior(s) did/do I use?

In the EMSO Foundations, you became aware of the Emotionally-Triggered Behaviors that are an unconscious reaction to people, groups, and situations in your life.

Now, get specific with which ETB(s) is at play with each person, group, and situation on your EMSO Master Chart.

Fill in Column E: ETB with the specific behavior(s) you displayed. Use the code(s) from the key on page 91.

The emotion I felt compelled me to behave in this way with this person, group, or in this situation:

_____

_____ .

BLAME

Do I still blame them or myself?

Fill in Column F: BLAME, indicating why you blame the person, group, or situation, and/or if you blame yourself for what happened.

I blame

_____

_____

for my PANEs because

_____

_____ .

EXPECTATION

Did I have any expectations? (spoken or unspoken)

Fill in Column G: EXPECTATIONS with specifics about what the expectations are or were with each person, group, or situation on your EMSO Master Chart. Indicate if these were spoken or unspoken.

I had/have expectations of

_____

_____ ,

which specifically include

_____

_____ .

MOTIVE

What did I hope to accomplish?

Fill in Column H: MOTIVE with an explanation of what you were hoping to accomplish by using the ETBs that you did with each person, group, or situation.

I behaved this way in order to

_____

_____

After your first past, look at each name/situation a second time and deeply ponder what you were thinking at the time of the event or during the relationship. Why did you truly do what you did? What motivated your behavior?

CONSEQUENCE

What happened next?

Fill in Column I: CONSEQUENCE with an explanation of what happened next. Did you lose anything? Did things remain the same?

After my experience with this person, group, or situation, this happened next:

_____

_____ .

REWIND

It's now time to name and claim: <u>What's my part in each situation?</u> You find this by asking yourself, "What would I now do differently?"

Fill in Column J: REWIND with the answer to that question for each person or group on your EMSO MASTER CHART. To support you in better understanding what you would now do differently, read the examples here:

HINT:

- *This isn't about regret, this is simply about rewinding and practicing making new decisions using old events!*

- I would be honest.

- I would think more about them.

- I wouldn't have expectations.

- I wouldn't judge them or be hypocritical.

- I would communciate more.

- I wouldn't emotionally manipulate.

- I wouldn't follow along with the crowd.

- I would love more openly rather than be so fearful and attached.

- I wouldn't express my anger in that way.

- I wouldn't keep that harmful secret.

- Other: _____

_____

_____

_____

_____

_____

_____

_____

_____

_____

_____

MY PART = MY RESPONSIBILITY

Take this opportunity to reflect on the lines on your EMSO MASTER CHART that surprised you the most when you realized that you actually had a part in creating the situation. Take responsibility in a new way and notice the freedom that comes with it. Write them here and on additional pieces of paper as needed.

We're all the same.

You're not alone.

"I acknowledge that the part I played in the experience with (person, group, or situation) _____ was _____ . I now take responsibility for my part in this."

"I acknowledge that the part I played in the experience with (person, group, or situation) _____ was _____ . I now take responsibility for my part in this."

"I acknowledge that the part I played in the experience with (person, group, or situation) _____ was _____ . I now take responsibility for my part in this."

"I acknowledge that the part I played in the experience with (person, group, or situation) _____ was _____ . I now take responsibility for my part in this."

"I acknowledge that the part I played in the experience with (person, group, or situation) _____ was _____ . I now take responsibility for my part in this."

"I acknowledge that the part I played in the experience with (person, group, or situation) _____ was _____ . I now take responsibility for my part in this."

"I acknowledge that the part I played in the experience with (person, group, or situation) _____ was _____ . I now take responsibility for my part in this."

"I acknowledge that the part I played in the experience with (person, group, or situation) _____ was _____ . I now take responsibility for my part in this."

SUMMARY OF EMSO INVESTIGATIONS: THE *YOU* YOU'VE NEVER NOTICED

Whether you're doing your EMSO Training via the online course, with a live group, through EMSO coaching, or reading "The *You* You've Never Met" as your primary guide, if you've made it here, you've taken the bold step of acknowledging who you've been being. Take some time to reflect on your EMSO INVESTIGATIONS, and free-write and/or draw below before moving on. Exhale.

EMSO REPAIRS

THE *YOU* YOU'RE REVEALING

INTRODUCTION TO EMSO REPAIRS: THE *YOU* YOU'RE REVEALING

You can change more of your past than you may think. This is especially true with EMSO Training. Your guilt, shame, regret, and all of your PANE can be healed with the right perspective and effort. You've done so much already, and now, the EMSO Community challenges you to make repairs by using what you've learned in this process thus far— some of your new maturity, clarity, and understanding of who you've been being, what's happened to you, and your new choice for yourself.

Like the oxygen mask on an airplane, you must first repair yourself before you can have the stability and sobriety to repair outwardly. Knowing this, you may now begin the 4Rs. The image of a strand of DNA represents how this process pieces together your life story until now, and allows you to repair it in order to live a life of your true potential, with levelheadedness, clarity, and peace.

THE REAL ME, PART 3: BLUEPRINT OF THE REAL ME

In the left-hand column, rewrite the most obvious Trauma-Influenced Self-Beliefs, Trauma Filters, and Emotionally-Triggered Behaviors (ETBs) that have made up your past.

For lack of a better term, these will be looked at as your "past weaknesses."

In the right-hand column, write what you perceive to be the opposite beliefs, filters, and behaviors as "new strengths." These will replace your old ways of being and will become your starting point in training to remember and continuously choose the real you, thus forming your chosen identity.

HINT: Your weakest and seemingly most negative traits are actually manifesting on the same plane as their opposites (potential replacements!), meaning these profoundly new and more beneficial qualities can become your greatest strengths.

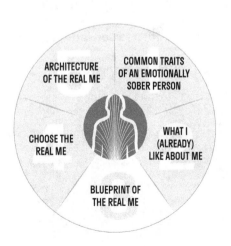

PAST "WEAKNESSES" (Self-Beliefs, Trauma Filters, and ETBs)	NEW "STRENGTHS" (Replacement Beliefs/Filters/Behaviors)

LEVELHEADEDDOC

REVIEW: PAINT MY PATTERNS

This exercise will clearly reveal the tendencies you portrayed within the situations and with the people on your EMSO MASTER CHART.

Use highlighters or colored pencils and color-code Columns C, D, & E. Choose one color for each BELIEF/FILTER, each PANE, and each ETB. You may choose to use the same color palette for all three columns, because we're looking only for patterns within each column.

For example:

- in Column C – BELIEF/FILTER: "UW" is also blue, "L/P" red, and "IA" yellow

- in Column D – PANE: "F" could be blue, "E" red, and "R" yellow

- in Column E – ETB: "DF" blue, "CH" red, and "JL" yellow

By clearly labelling each with a color, you'll be able to see a visual display of certain destructive patterns. For example, if you use blue for all your fears and you see a lot of blue in Column D, you'll have a clearer sense of how much fear has been influencing your life.

Do you see any colorful patterns? Do these match your Anatomy of Emotional Insobriety (see page 43)?

REVIEW: HIGHLIGHT WHAT NEEDS REPAIRING WITHIN ME

Next, get a highlighter and review each person, group, and situation you wrote in Column A: NAME on your EMSO MASTER CHART.

Highlight the name for any that you feel the following when you review.

- PANE (resentment, anger, guilt, embarrassment, fear, or sadness)

- Body Signals (Do you feel uneasy when you think of them?)

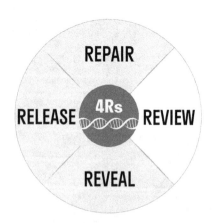

REVEAL: MY INTOXICATED IDENTITY

Now that you've reviewed all of the components of your emotional insobriety that have created or are adding to the problems in your life, reveal them to yourself in a very direct and loving way. This is who you became because of Early-Age Trauma.

Read your entire EMSO MASTER CHART <u>out loud</u> to yourself.

Take the time to really acknowledge the things you've done, failed to do, or what happened to you in your childhood that formed your Intoxicated Identity.

Then respond to these prompts:

1. I acknowledge my patterns of:

_____

_____

_____

2. I could have saved myself and others from unnecessary pain by:

_____

_____

3. These Predominant Accompanying Negative Emotions (PANEs), Trauma Filters, and Emotionally-Triggered Behaviors (ETBs) have been my biggest blocks:

_____

_____

_____

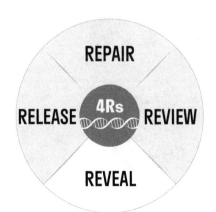

REVEAL: WHO I'VE REALLY BEEN BEING

This is a unique opportunity and freeing exercise to reveal your biggest secrets, lies, and overall Intoxicated Identity to someone else.

- OPTION 1: Reveal your Intoxicated Identity (what you uncovered on your EMSO MASTER CHART) to an EMSO Coach, to the EMSO Community (on the group page or in a meeting), or to your EMSO CO.

- OPTION 2: Choose a truly trusted person to talk to—a rabbi, teacher, mentor, clergyman, therapist, counselor, or the like. Ask for a meeting to express what you found in your EMSO MASTER CHART and any revelations you've had about who you've been being.

Remind yourself that this exercise isn't about the therapy or advice you will receive from others; it's simply another human being that you can reveal these secrets to. It's a place for you to humbly purge your past. Once you've finished revealing to them, do not engage in much discussion, unless you need support from a professional mental health practitioner.

HINT: Some people have a hard time revealing due to fearing judgment. Remember, to whom you choose to confess is only an ear, not a judge.

RELEASE: THE OLD TO MEET THE FUTURE

Visit **liftedacademy.com/tyynm** and listen to the recording, "Release." Lay in a comfortable location, close your eyes, and listen deeply. Remove all distractions ahead of time.

Notice if your heart begins to swell as if you've just watched an inspiring or heartfelt movie. This is your energy touching you.

Once you feel confident that you're surrounded by it, declare your readiness and read the statement to the right.

Then, take some time to free-write and/or draw how you feel and what you notice.

"I'm ready for the energy that made and keeps me to help me remove and destroy my hurtful compulsions, my past pain, my anger, my guilt, and my belligerence.

I release this and ask that you remove every hurtful compulsion, my past pain, my anger, my guilt, and my belligerence. Remove everything that stands in the way of my usefulness and peace, and let me outgrow fear."

Visualize this actually happening in real time. Feel space freeing up inside of you. Feel yourself getting lighter, freer, and emptier as these things leave you.

Then say, "Thank you."

Say it only when you mean it, and feel it with humility. Stay in this moment for as long as you can. Continue to feel the blocks from your old self getting removed as the real you begins to shine through.

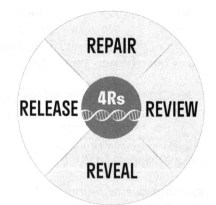

REPAIR: WRITE REPAIR FROM WITHIN LETTERS

Using this template, translate the contents of your EMSO MASTER CHART into one letter per person, group, or situation. Start by addressing each NAME you highlighted. These letters are for you, so don't write them as if someone will read it.

You can address each portion of your letter by looking at the respective columns on your EMSO MASTER CHART, indicated by the letter in the outline.

For example, [C] is found in the BELIEF/FILTER column, [E] is the ETB you displayed, etc.

Use this template as a guide to write your letters, yet make sure each one is written from your own voice, and that you truly mean it. Use your humility, modesty, and honesty. Ensure you're coming from a place of new maturity.

HINTS:

- *Use stationary or a dedicated note-book and find a quiet place without time pressure.*

- *Read the example letter in the book, "The You You've Never Met."*

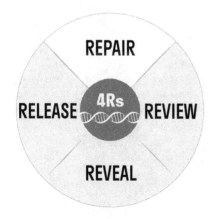

- **Address the letter.** Dear [A:_____],

- **Begin the letter by stating your intention.** I intend to clarify what I've learned about myself and our relationship/the situation.

- **Share the situation.** At the time [B:_____] happened...

- **Indicate your belief and/or filter.** This situation was difficult for me because I believed it meant [C:_____] about me, and I recognize that I filtered this situation through this lens.

- **Share your PANE around the situation.** Due to this belief seemingly being validated during this situation with you, I felt [D:_____].

- **Write down your ETBs.** These feelings in me caused me to behave [E:_____]. I specifically behaved this way by_____.

- **If you had any blame and/or expectations** [F/G], communicate this in the letter.

- **Reveal your motive.** By behaving this way, I was hoping to accomplish [H:_____].

- **Share what happened next.** I recognize the natural consequence of this is/was [I:_____].

- **Rewind.** What I would now do differently is [J:_____].

The last four parts of the letter aren't derived from your EMSO Master Chart, rather through The Real Me process and the skills you're developing with the EMSO Choices (understanding, acceptance, etc.)

- **State your new intentions.** I've chosen to be [emotionally sober traits, new strengths, etc.]_____ from now on.

- **Communicate that there are no lingering expectations.** As I'm sharing this, I realize that I don't have any expectations of you.

- **Express your gratitude.** You added _____ to my life. This situation or discord brought to light _____, which I'm now thankful for.

- **Close the letter** respectfully and modestly, with no emotional leverage. With respect, _____.

LEVELS OF REPAIRS

After you've written your Repair from Within Letters, you may notice that you want to reach out and make additional efforts toward healing your relationships, using your newfound humility. For now, keep the letters to yourself and use this chart to write in the names of people you may eventually wish to repair with in other ways. This will aid you in preparing for the more advanced step of Indirect and Direct Repairs, which you will learn in future trainings.

LEVEL 1: REPAIRS FROM WITHIN	LEVEL 2: INDIRECT REPAIRS			LEVEL 3: DIRECT REPAIRS		
Write Letter (not sent)	Action-based	Hand-written letter	Email	Phone call	Video call	Meet in person

WHO AM I NOW?

Now that you've complete all of the Take Actions and your EMSO MASTER CHART, write a letter to yourself now.

It's a moment to take a new "snapshot" of where you are in your EMSO journey. How do you feel day to day in your life right now?

You may choose to paste in a current photo as well.

Dear Me Now,

_____

_____

_____

_____

_____

_____

_____

_____

_____

_____

_____

_____

_____

_____

_____

_____

_____

Always here for you,

Me

SUMMARY OF EMSO REPAIRS: THE *YOU* YOU'RE REVEALING

If you've done the work to this point, these 4Rs may have already begun healing your life with the humility that they've required. They've allowed you to slowly and deliberately Review your Anatomy of Emotional Insobriety and EMSO Master Chart, and Reveal who you've been being to yourself and at least one other person. You gave yourself the opportunity to experience an initial Release of your ETBs, Beliefs, and PANEs, and you've written a Repair From Within letter for at least one person on your EMSO Master Chart. Allow each of these experiences to change you, to grow you, to support you in becoming the *you* you've never met.

Take a few minutes to reflect on this section as you complete this third and final portion of your EMSO Essentials:

IN CLOSING...

What an incredible journey you've just taken!

You completed the EMSO Essentials Take Actions and learned how to use the EMSO Master Chart—skills that will greatly serve your ongoing EMSO Training.

If you completed this journal on your own while reading "The *You* You've Never Met," you may find that going through EMSO Training in a more supported environment will help deepen your process, sustain your Emotional Sobriety, and be more fun! To continue with me and the larger support community, visit: **liftedacademy.com**

If you completed this journal and the EMSO Essentials via an online course, join the EMSO Practicum where we put all of your newly acquired skills into daily practice. The EMSO Practicum also teaches you new skills and the practical application of EMSO Training within all of your relationships. You'll also learn how to navigate through the things you may be coming up against as an EMSO Trainee.

Lastly, share this with your friends and family, and together let's add more Emotional Sobriety to the world, one brave and gritty person at a time! Visit your member page for simple ways to invite others to begin their journey: **liftedacademy.com/tyynm**

Always here for you,

Dr. Andrea Vitz

LEVELHEADEDDOC.COM

EMSO MASTER CHARTS

BLANK TEMPLATES

KEY: EMSO MASTER CHART

COLUMN C: BELIEF / FILTER

D= "I'm not safe" / Danger

CH= "I don't get a choice" / Choicelessness

VC= "I can't have a voice" / Voicelessness

NV= "I have little to offer" / Non-Value

DFT= "I can't do it" / Defeatism

DT= "I'm going to be betrayed/tricked" / Distrust

AR= "I can do no wrong" / Arrogance

PR= "I have to be perfect to be loved" / Perfection

TR= "I'm going to be punished/get in trouble" / Trouble

SH= "I'm a bad person" / Shamefulness

IA= "I'm not good enough" / Inadequacy

UW= "I don't deserve _____" / Unworthiness

UF= "It's not fair!" / Unfairness

UL= "Nobody loves me" / Unlovability

UNA= "I'm disgusting" / Unattractiveness

CAP= "I can't commit; I'll get trapped" / Captivity

UI= "I don't matter; I don't want to be a burden" / Unimportance

VM= "Bad things happen to me" / Victimhood

WND= "I can't change what happened to me" / Woundedness

PV= "I can't make enough money" / Poverty

L= "I can't have what I want" / Lack

ALN= "I'm alone in the world" / Aloneness

FR= "I'm breakable" / Fragility

IV= "Nobody sees me" / Invisibility

DP= "I can't feel joy" / Depression

D/S= "I have many things wrong with me" / Dis-ease/Sickness

F= "It's all my fault" / Fault

BL= "It's never my fault" / Blame

COR= "I'm damaged, 'sinful,' or impure" / Corruption

OB= "I don't need any help; I'm fine!" / Obstinance

ES= "I need an escape; I need alcohol, drugs, food, etc. to cope" / Escapism

DTA= "I can't love" / Detachment

UNT= "They think I'm stupid" / Unintelligence

RJ= "I'm going to be rejected" / Rejection

Additional: _____

_____

_____

_____

_____

_____

_____

_____

COLUMN D: PREDOMINANT ACCOMPANYING EMOTION (PANE)

R= Resentment

A= Anger

G= Guilt

E= Embarrassment

F= Fear

S= Sadness

COLUMN E: EMOTIONALLY-TRIGGERED BEHAVIOR (ETB)

DF= Defensiveness

CH= Childishness

JL= Jealousy

SC= Self-Centeredness

JG= Judgmentalism

DH= Dishonesty

SA= Secondary Addiction

A NAME	B SITUATION	C BELIEF/FILTER	D PANE	E ETB
Who have I hurt? Who's hurt me? (person or event)	What happened?	What does this mean about me?	What emotion do I feel?	How did I/am I behaving?
			R A G E F S	
			R A G E F S	
			R A G E F S	
			R A G E F S	
			R A G E F S	
			R A G E F S	

R=RESENTMENT   A=ANGER   G=GUILT   E=EMBARRASSMENT   F=FEAR   S=SADNESS

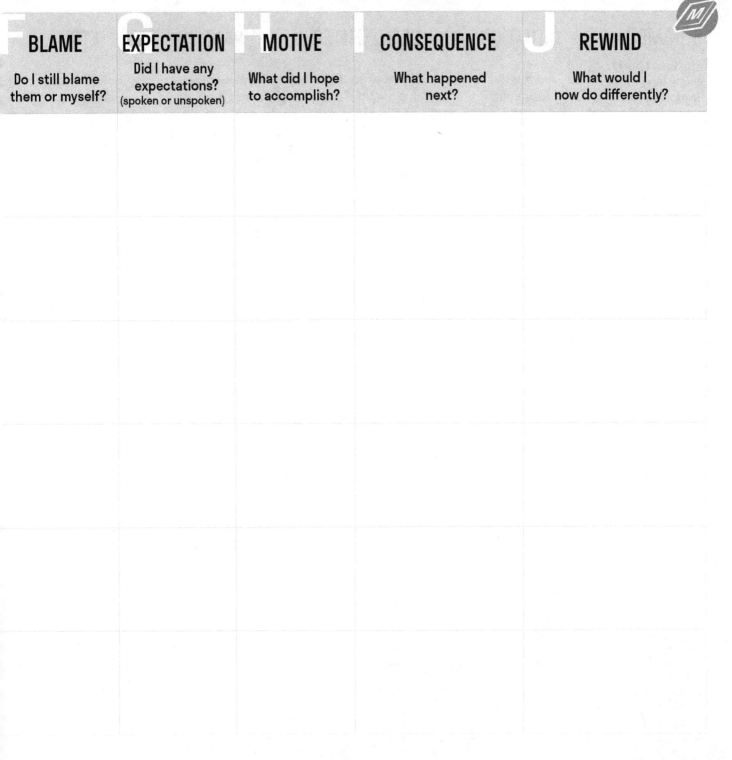

F BLAME	G EXPECTATION	H MOTIVE	I CONSEQUENCE	J REWIND
Do I still blame them or myself?	Did I have any expectations? (spoken or unspoken)	What did I hope to accomplish?	What happened next?	What would I now do differently?

A NAME	**B** SITUATION	**C** BELIEF/FILTER	**D** PANE	**E** ETB
Who have I hurt? Who's hurt me? (person or event)	What happened?	What does this mean about me?	What emotion do I feel?	How did I/am I behaving?
			R A G E F S	
			R A G E F S	
			R A G E F S	
			R A G E F S	
			R A G E F S	
			R A G E F S	

R=RESENTMENT   A=ANGER   G=GUILT   E=EMBARRASSMENT   F=FEAR   S=SADNESS

F BLAME	G EXPECTATION	H MOTIVE	I CONSEQUENCE	J REWIND
Do I still blame them or myself?	Did I have any expectations? (spoken or unspoken)	What did I hope to accomplish?	What happened next?	What would I now do differently?

A NAME	B SITUATION	C BELIEF/FILTER	D PANE	E ETB
Who have I hurt? Who's hurt me? (person or event)	What happened?	What does this mean about me?	What emotion do I feel?	How did I/am I behaving?
			R A G E F S	
			R A G E F S	
			R A G E F S	
			R A G E F S	
			R A G E F S	
			R A G E F S	

R=RESENTMENT   A=ANGER   G=GUILT   E=EMBARRASSMENT   F=FEAR   S=SADNESS

F BLAME	G EXPECTATION	H MOTIVE	I CONSEQUENCE	J REWIND
Do I still blame them or myself?	Did I have any expectations? (spoken or unspoken)	What did I hope to accomplish?	What happened next?	What would I now do differently?

A NAME	**B** SITUATION	**C** BELIEF/FILTER	**D** PANE	**E** ETB
Who have I hurt? Who's hurt me? (person or event)	What happened?	What does this mean about me?	What emotion do I feel?	How did I/am I behaving?
			R A G E F S	
			R A G E F S	
			R A G E F S	
			R A G E F S	
			R A G E F S	
			R A G E F S	

R=RESENTMENT   A=ANGER   G=GUILT   E=EMBARRASSMENT   F=FEAR   S=SADNESS

F BLAME	**G** EXPECTATION	**H** MOTIVE	**I** CONSEQUENCE	**J** REWIND
Do I still blame them or myself?	Did I have any expectations? (spoken or unspoken)	What did I hope to accomplish?	What happened next?	What would I now do differently?

A NAME	B SITUATION	BELIEF/FILTER	D PANE	E ETB
Who have I hurt? Who's hurt me? (person or event)	What happened?	What does this mean about me?	What emotion do I feel?	How did I/am I behaving?
			R A G E F S	
			R A G E F S	
			R A G E F S	
			R A G E F S	
			R A G E F S	
			R A G E F S	

R=RESENTMENT   A=ANGER   G=GUILT   E=EMBARRASSMENT   F=FEAR   S=SADNESS

F BLAME	G EXPECTATION	H MOTIVE	I CONSEQUENCE	J REWIND
Do I still blame them or myself?	Did I have any expectations? (spoken or unspoken)	What did I hope to accomplish?	What happened next?	What would I now do differently?

A NAME Who have I hurt? Who's hurt me? (person or event)	B SITUATION What happened?	C BELIEF/FILTER What does this mean about me?	D PANE What emotion do I feel?	E ETB How did I/am I behaving?
			R A G E F S	
			R A G E F S	
			R A G E F S	
			R A G E F S	
			R A G E F S	
			R A G E F S	

R=RESENTMENT   A=ANGER   G=GUILT   E=EMBARRASSMENT   F=FEAR   S=SADNESS

F BLAME	**G** EXPECTATION	**H** MOTIVE	**I** CONSEQUENCE	**J** REWIND
Do I still blame them or myself?	Did I have any expectations? (spoken or unspoken)	What did I hope to accomplish?	What happened next?	What would I now do differently?

A NAME	B SITUATION	C BELIEF/FILTER	D PANE	E ETB
Who have I hurt? Who's hurt me? (person or event)	What happened?	What does this mean about me?	What emotion do I feel?	How did I/am I behaving?
			R A G E F S	
			R A G E F S	
			R A G E F S	
			R A G E F S	
			R A G E F S	
			R A G E F S	

R=RESENTMENT   A=ANGER   G=GUILT   E=EMBARRASSMENT   F=FEAR   S=SADNESS

F BLAME	G EXPECTATION	H MOTIVE	I CONSEQUENCE	J REWIND
Do I still blame them or myself?	Did I have any expectations? (spoken or unspoken)	What did I hope to accomplish?	What happened next?	What would I now do differently?

A NAME	**B** SITUATION	**C** BELIEF/FILTER	**D** PANE	**E** ETB
Who have I hurt? Who's hurt me? (person or event)	What happened?	What does this mean about me?	What emotion do I feel?	How did I/am I behaving?
			R A G E F S	
			R A G E F S	
			R A G E F S	
			R A G E F S	
			R A G E F S	
			R A G E F S	

R=RESENTMENT   A=ANGER   G=GUILT E=EMBARRASSMENT F=FEAR S=SADNESS

F BLAME	G EXPECTATION	H MOTIVE	I CONSEQUENCE	J REWIND
Do I still blame them or myself?	Did I have any expectations? (spoken or unspoken)	What did I hope to accomplish?	What happened next?	What would I now do differently?

A NAME	**B** SITUATION	**C** BELIEF/FILTER	**D** PANE	**E** ETB
Who have I hurt? Who's hurt me? (person or event)	What happened?	What does this mean about me?	What emotion do I feel?	How did I/am I behaving?
			R A G E F S	
			R A G E F S	
			R A G E F S	
			R A G E F S	
			R A G E F S	
			R A G E F S	

R=RESENTMENT   A=ANGER   G=GUILT   E=EMBARRASSMENT   F=FEAR   S=SADNESS

F BLAME	**G** EXPECTATION	**H** MOTIVE	**I** CONSEQUENCE	**J** REWIND
Do I still blame them or myself?	Did I have any expectations? (spoken or unspoken)	What did I hope to accomplish?	What happened next?	What would I now do differently?

A NAME	**B** SITUATION	**C** BELIEF/FILTER	**D** PANE	**E** ETB
Who have I hurt? Who's hurt me? (person or event)	What happened?	What does this mean about me?	What emotion do I feel?	How did I/am I behaving?
			R A G E F S	
			R A G E F S	
			R A G E F S	
			R A G E F S	
			R A G E F S	
			R A G E F S	

R=RESENTMENT   A=ANGER   G=GUILT   E=EMBARRASSMENT   F=FEAR   S=SADNESS

F BLAME	G EXPECTATION	H MOTIVE	I CONSEQUENCE	J REWIND
Do I still blame them or myself?	Did I have any expectations? (spoken or unspoken)	What did I hope to accomplish?	What happened next?	What would I now do differently?

The *You* You've Never Met Companion Journal, Revised Edition

Copyright © 2021 Dr. Andrea Vitz

ISBN: 978-1-7344090-2-4

Author: Dr. Andrea Vitz

Editor: Amanda Kay Creighton

Illustrator: Dustin Eli Brunson

Revised printing edition 2021. Vitz, Andrea

Trademark: The *You* You've Never Met

CPSIA information can be obtained
at www.ICGtesting.com
Printed in the USA
LVHW052255111222
735022LV00029B/1254